Prince of Wentworth Street

An American boyhood in the shadow of a genocide

John Christie

PLAIDSWEDE PUBLISHING
Concord, New Hampshire

Prince of Wentworth Street: An American boyhood in the shadow of a genocide

Printed in the United States of America

ISBN: 978-1-7333556-7-4

Published by:
Plaidswede Publishing
P.O. Box 269 Concord, New Hampshire 03302-0269

www.plaidswede.com

Front and back cover photo credits of John Christie: Naomi Schalit
Map design: Dragonfly Studio

"In this intensely personal memoir, Christie arrives at a moment of inexplicable dread late in life that forces him to peel back layers of identity — designated good boy, journalist and businessman.

His mission is to find his true self, and the journey leads back to the poor mill town where he grew up and to his grandmother, a survivor of the Armenian genocide who made a life in America.

This is a book that will appeal to all readers interested in families and the ways which the children of immigrant families make themselves into Americans."

> — Lou Ureneck, journalism professor at Boston University and award-winning author of *Smyrna, September 1922.*

"This beautifully told story is both ageless and modern — coming to understand that your identity is defined by both genocide and survival."

> — Stephen Kurkjian, three-times winner of the Pulitzer Prize in journalism and son of a survivor of the Armenian Genocide.

Christie's poignant and beautifully written memoir begins with a murder in an ancient land and ends there a century later with Christie plucking a leaf from a mulberry tree, a symbol of the gratitude he owed his family.

Above all, *Prince of Wentworth Street* is a story of loyalty to family, to heritage and to the ideals that helped a lost man find his way back home.

> — Barbara Walsh, Pulitzer Prize-winning journalist and author of *August Gale: A Father and Daughter's Journey into the Storm* and *Sammy in the Sky.*

Dedication

To Nick and Naomi

Table of Contents

Dedication .... *v*

Acknowledgments.. *ix*

Reverie .... *xiii*

Introduction .... *xv*

CHAPTER 1   Foreigner.. *1*

CHAPTER 2   The Tammy tape *8*

CHAPTER 3   "They're killing the kefir"............................... *13*

CHAPTER 4   Bread and cucumbers *23*

CHAPTER 5   "Gonna burn us to death"............................... *29*

CHAPTER 6   A heart in pieces *33*

CHAPTER 7   From Cairo to America.................................. *37*

CHAPTER 8   Johnny's here! *42*

CHAPTER 9   The boy in the cashmere coat *48*

CHAPTER 10   Scout's honor *55*

CHAPTER 11   A man named Licky *62*

CHAPTER 12   Up from the tenement *68*

CHAPTER 13   Mack's wild ride *71*

CHAPTER 14   How to build a basketball court..................... *76*

CHAPTER 15   Wooden nickels... *80*

CHAPTER 16   Mrs. Mack drove the getaway car................... *85*

CHAPTER 17   A medal for Boris... *92*

CHAPTER 18   Incident on Niles Street *98*

CHAPTER 19   Caught stealing... *106*

CHAPTER 20   The boy and the casket *109*

CHAPTER 21   The best years of her life............................... *118*

CHAPTER 22   Oh, brother *122*

CHAPTER 23   The line breaks *126*

CHAPTER 24   Dover to Boston to The Haight *133*

CHAPTER 25   One blissful moment..................................... *139*

CHAPTER 26   Freedom came too late *144*

CHAPTER 27   The Professor calls home............................... *149*

CHAPTER 28   Encounter with Tammy *157*

CHAPTER 29   Return to Suedia *164*

Epilogue.. *177*

Bibliography.. *178*

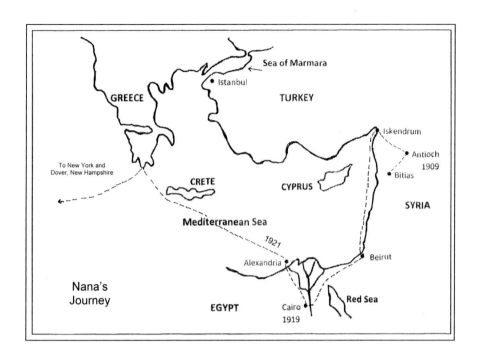

Nana's Journey

Acknowledgments

"What do you do when your mother tells you she loves you?"
"Check it out."

That's one of the first lessons I got as a newspaper reporter starting my career in the early 1970s. Yes, it was cynical and these days perhaps not terribly politic, but few of us ever forgot the point. Thus, even when the subject is yourself, you have to find ways to check it out.

Among those who patiently endured my questioning were family and friends: Aunts Lillian (Aunt Lity) Goodman, Mary (Army Mae) McKenney and Nancy Banaian; Uncle George "Joe" Banaian; cousins King Banaian, Jodi Goodman, Dean Banaian, Vicky (Banaian) Connell and Douglas Brooks; friends James "Mack" McEneaney, Kevin McEneaney, Pat Boyle and Ginny Christie.

Cousin Tammy Fareed not only opened up about her immediate family, but without her recorded interview with Nana, there would not have been a book at all.

I am grateful to my writerly friends who gave me candid and invaluable comments on early drafts: Gail Kelly, Andy Merton, Sharron Cohen, Dave Cohen, Hallie Herz and Jane Harrigan. Beth Rashbaum of Independent Editors Group provided a professional book editor's evaluation, from hard-nosed line edits to demands to get the big picture right. Rick Lawrence's eagle eye caught many an error.

Fellow Armenians, journalists, authors and friends who provided advice and encouragement include Steve Kurkjian, Nubar Alexanian, Quil Lawrence, Rick and Sandra Lawrence, Matt Storin, George Geers (also my publisher), Lou Ureneck, Barbara Walsh, Raffi Der Simonian, Arlie and Adam Hochschild, Lee McIntyre, Dover native Marc A. Mamigonian, director of academic affairs at the National Association of Armenian Studies and Research and the late Warren Watson. Thanks, too, to Judy Davison for the elegant design.

Two editors were gracious enough to publish my shorter versions of Nana's story: Greg Kesich of the Maine Sunday Telegram and Portland Press Herald and Cloe Axelson of WBUR's Cognoscenti magazine.

Without the guidance of Annie Kahkejian of Historic Armenia tours and her driver, Seljuk, Nick and I would never have found Nana's village. Whatever the challenge on our trip to Turkey, they came through with good cheer and patience.

My son, Nicholas Christie, put his English degree to good use editing every word in the book and saving me from many writing sins, especially the run-on sentence. He also funded a good part of the trip to Turkey where I occasionally violated my promise to him to be discreet in my questioning.

It would take another chapter to list all the ways my wife, the journalist Naomi Schalit, is the reason this book went from poorly-formed concept to a completed manuscript. She edited at least six drafts. Her editing went well beyond a professional critique of words, sentences and paragraphs. What made the book come together was her insistence that I not just tell the story, but feel the story, as painful as that was sometimes.

Except for the names of two people that were changed to protect their privacy, the rest checks out as well as my memory has allowed.

"Midway through the journey of my life I found myself within a dark forest/for the straightforward path had been lost."

— Dante

"I should have thought that was why one wrote — to make something useful for the survivors, to say: I was and now you are, and I leave as good a map as I could make of my own traveling."

— Gore Vidal

My Family

Mariam Boyajian
Born Turkey
Died 1918

Elias Hovsepian
Born Turkey
Died 1909

Gulenia (Rose) Hovsepian
Born Turkey
1899-1995

John Banaian
Born Turkey
1889-1933

Elias (Dean) Banaian
Born Dover, NH
1925-1958

Stephen (Licky) Banaian
Born Dover, NH
1926-1998

Koharig Banaian
Born Dover, NH
1923-2002

Thomas Christie
Born Dover, NH
1912-1967

George (Joe) Banaian
Born Dover, NH
1927-2017

Mary (Army Mae)
Banian
Born Dover, NH
1929-

Lillian (Lil, Aunty Lily)
Banaian
Born Dover, NH
1930-

Naomi Schalit
Born Southampton, NY
1957-

John Christie
Born Dover, NH
1948-

Janet (Glony) Pinsince
Born Dover, NH
1947-2017

Gary Christie
Born Dover, NH
1951-2002

Nicholas (Nick)
Christie
Born Gloucester, MA
1980-

Note: Lillian (Banaian) Goodman has two children, Jody and Jeff; Mary (Banaian) McKenny has one daughter, Cindy; George Banaian is survived by his wife, Nancy, and three children. King, Vicky and Dean. My wife, Naomi Schalit, has two children, Nat and Hallie Herz.

Reverie

My feet, clad in black Converse sneakers, stand astride the manhole cover at the far end of the basketball court erected by the Henry Law Avenue gang on a side street. I am the new boy, and the others look at how far away I am from the basket and shake their heads or curl their lips in a "no way" expression.

I lick my fingers, as I always did, to get a firmer grip on the basketball. I center the nubbled ball by its east-west axis, bend my knees deep for extra power, focus my eyes on the back of the rim and set a course with a high trajectory so the ball will drop cleanly through the net, snapping it upwards from the friction of rubber on corded cotton.

The ball is airborne, 15, 20 feet above the rutted asphalt, above the heads of boys in white t-shirts, carrying the hopes of the prince of Wentworth Street to shed that title and become just one of the guys.

Christie, in 1980, in the State House press room in Boston, where he was a correspondent for six Massachusetts daily newspapers. Photo by Charles A. Lowe.

Introduction

"Who made us?"
— The first line in the Baltimore Catechism

For my entire writing life, I was a reporter. I wrote about city council meetings and presidential campaigns; I dug up stories about police brutality and government fraud; I composed features about Boston's street people and antiquarian bookstores. Once I even wrote a travel piece about climbing Caribbean peaks.

The work always began the same way. Start with the facts: Calculate the increase in the city's budget. Get quotes from the mayor and city councilors. Interview some homeowners. Organize my notes. Fill in the blanks with more interviews. Write.

This writing was different.

Writing about your own life is an attempt to unearth some essential truth, and the truth is more than a summary of facts — names, votes, stats, quotes. Those were relatively easy to come by when I was a newspaper reporter. But the truth of a life comes from a deeper place. For me it is a place that relies on memories constructed from snippets of conversations with my mother, the chalk dust on Sister Aloysius's black habit, the amber glow off that first glass of beer, the only epithet I have heard my grandmother speak — "You dirty Turk" — and a tape recording I'd not known existed until I began to write this book. Someone else might say it was Sister Monica who always had chalk dust on her habit or that I never drank that offered beer. Whether I drank that beer is not the point because my belief in who I was then and who I am now stands on a foundation built from these memories, these stories, which I can still see and hear and smell when I close my eyes and travel to the past.

Lewis Thomas, in his essay, "A Long Line of Cells," wrote of his memories: "A surprising number turn out to be wishes, rather than recollections, hopes that the place really did work the way everyone said it was supposed to work, hankerings that the one thing leading to another has a direction of some kind, and a hope for a pattern from the jumble — an epiphany out of entropy."

Each of my recollections — or perhaps they are wishes — arrives with the hope that it will connect with the others, each becoming its own small epiphany to tell a full story of who made me.

Photo by Jan Norman.

CHAPTER 1

Foreigner

"Stop the car, Naomi. Right here, pull over. I have to get out."

We were somewhere in Ontario, Canada, returning home to Maine from visiting Naomi's daughter at her summer camp. The trip had not gone well. Naomi, the woman I was living with, wanted me to share this part of her life, her annual trip to a deep woods canoe camp where her daughter and son spent most summers, taking long — sometimes weeks-long — canoeing adventures. Hallie had become so adept she was now leading some of these trips. We had driven the two days to the camp to be there in time for the ceremonial return of Hallie's "trippers" from their 30-day excursion into the wilderness.

With the hope that our relationship would lead to marriage — a second marriage for both of us — Naomi and I wanted to "be known" by each other. For Naomi, that meant my appreciating her connection to the camp because it had helped shape her children into strong, independent and confident young adults, and there was nothing more important in her life than her daughter and son.

I was just becoming acquainted with Hallie, who was 23, and Nat, 25. They had treated the new man in their mother's life with generosity, kindness and openness. I was aware that they had a good dad already; my role was to love their mother and be kind and open to them, which would not be hard to do.

Naomi wanted me to understand that this was no country-club camp for the privileged; that, as a single mother, she had found this camp, arranged for her kids to start there as rank beginners, watched as they progressed to become expert paddlers and campers, and felt an earned sense of pride in their successes. She thought I would be as thrilled as she was at Hallie's achievements, and would revel in the peaceful beauty of the trees, the lakes and the star-filled sky.

But, the feelings Naomi was sure the visit would bring out in me — the feelings I, too, thought I would have — didn't materialize.

The moment when I should have had the peak experience occurs when the campers paddle in a row towards a small inlet where they can tie up their canoes and hug the families and friends who have been waiting to celebrate their return. The parents crowd a small wooden bridge that spans the entry to the inlet, smart phones at the ready to take photos and videos of the triumphal arrival. The kids wave their paddles and whoop it up and the parents, including Naomi, are ecstatic — yelling, clapping, calling out their kids' names and even crying.

When the campers glided under the bridge, I clapped and waved at Hallie because I knew that was the right and polite thing to do; but I didn't feel anything. I was going through the motions while being taken over by a sense of disassociation. My body was there, but the rest of me was elsewhere.

If I could feel what Naomi felt, if I could internalize the joy and the pride she felt, then, she said, I would truly know her. That felt fair to me, for she had already made the same effort for me by spending time in my hometown, seeing the now-decrepit tenement where I grew up, the mammoth brick mill where the fathers worked, the doughnut shop where I indulged in a honey-dip and a chocolate milk after playing basketball.

While she was already aware that I was in many ways her opposite — working class, Catholic, public university versus middle class, Jewish, Ivy League —I thought that seeing where I came from with her own eyes would make these abstractions real. I hadn't expected it would change her mind about me — I knew her too well to think of her as that shallow — still, it's one thing to be in a relationship with someone from such a different background, another thing to see it and still have faith that you can spend the rest of your lives together.

Like me, she wanted to be known by more than her resume — and the rough camp would be one way for me to do that.

• • •

On that late summer day in 2012 when we left the Maine home we had been sharing, I felt confident that's exactly what would happen, that I would be as interested in her experiences as she had been in mine.

To get to the camp, you drive a day from central Maine to Ottawa, stay overnight in a hotel, and then drive another day further north, seeing fewer and fewer other cars as you pass through the endless miles of pine woods that flank the road. Nothing about this was foreign to me. I had camped in the woods of New Hampshire and Maine many times, backpacked in the Southwest, driven 'cross country in a beat-up van. I could surely handle hanging around a rustic canoeing camp for a couple of days.

The camp's parking lot is just some empty spaces between trees. To get to the camp you hump your luggage a mile or so through the woods to a lake where modest timber buildings are spread out near the beach. The rudimentary camp is nothing more than a staging area. The campers provision, train there and then embark to remote lakes and rivers, testing themselves against rapids, portaging canoes and equipment across rough terrain, sleeping on rocky beaches, cooking for themselves and solving any problems that come up, from injuries to fears about negotiating raging waters, boulders and sandbars.

Naomi had been to the camp a dozen or more times over the years, and I saw that she quickly connected with the other parents, sharing stories of past trips, their children's friendships, anecdotes of near disasters and hilarious moments. The more exposed I was to their inside jokes and gossip, the more I felt left out, alienated.

This was not my social class: They were mostly well-off Canadians, members of the professional classes. Of course, as the recently retired president of a medium-sized publishing company, I was part of the same economic strata, and as an accomplished journalist, I was a professional. But what felt to me like an assumed air of privilege fired up the working class boy in me, the identity that is never too far from my surface.

They all seemed to come with the same profile: wealthy, well-bred environmentalists, hearty and fit, with a habit of drinking cocktails and eating cheeses I had never heard of.

I sensed they all had pedigrees. And I didn't.

Having reduced them to a stereotype and declared myself an unwelcome outsider, I felt isolated. So while Naomi and the other parents relived the stories of past canoe trips, of long-ago parties on the lakefront beach, I wandered off to the water's edge, where I sat on a log as the sky darkened along with my mood.

My attitude surprised me. And it scared me. A lot was riding on my reactions to this trip. Although all I had to do was enjoy myself and cheer on the kids, I couldn't even do that.

I didn't like these people, and I didn't like me for not liking them.

What was going on?

What was the big deal about the class and social differences? This sort of thing had rarely bothered me in the past. My very best friends — a couple I went to college with — couldn't have been more different from me: The husband came from an old-line family of bankers and his wife was upper middle class and Jewish. I found out later she and Naomi went to the same progressive elementary school in New York. All my professional life I had worked with people born and raised in much better circumstances than I had been, and I had never felt at odds with them.

Now, though, "traitor" was the word that kept coming to me.

Here I was in a country that was not mine, with a family that was not mine, with a class of people that was not mine.

I felt disloyal, and the longer I was exposed to this place where I was the outsider, the more I retreated within myself, the more my internal voice declared that I was betraying who I was in order to get something for myself — the approval of a woman I loved.

As Naomi drove us away from the camp, an icy grimness lay between us in the car. My retreat over the past days into a near-silent black hole — "I can't reach you in there, John" — had forced Naomi to divide her attention between my dark mood and her own pleasure at being reunited with her daughter. I said very little and began to take solace by staring into the deep, green forests that surrounded us. The idea took hold that if we could just pull over for awhile, I could walk into that forest and I'd be able to let go of all of the regrets and fears, the anxiety and resentment that were obstacles to embracing a new stage of life.

"Why? Why do you want to get out here? What's going on with you," Naomi asked as she slowed the car to a halt by the side of the road.

I didn't answer because I didn't know. I stepped out of the car, walked to the shoulder and looked as far into the distant forest as my eyes could focus. I breathed deeply, trying to tamp down a breathless anxiety, a jitteriness in my chest that scared me. I wanted to scream louder than is humanly possible, howl into those woods, but I didn't because it would have scared Naomi, and I thought I had already done enough damage to her.

A few more deep breaths and I got back in the car. I tried to explain myself and beg forgiveness. I offered to end the relationship if that's what she wanted.

"No," Naomi said, "but this can't happen again when I see my kids. You made it impossible for me to enjoy something that is so important in my life and my kids' lives."

In the end, we agreed that I needed to find out where these feelings came from.

While an audio book played on the car's sound system, the sonorous voice of the narrator lulled me into a near-trance, an introspective state where I began to consider my state of mind, to discover when I might have begun to feel estranged from myself.

In the previous two years, the roles by which I identified myself for most of my adult life had disappeared. My wife of 30-plus years asked for a divorce.

There went one of the roles that told me who I was — "husband."

Then my newspaper publishing company was sold because, as had happened at many media companies, the owners had taken on a level of debt that couldn't be sustained when the advertisers we counted on were moving to cheap internet ads. When new owners came in they eliminated my position as publisher and CEO — and there went another name I had for myself.

I was still a dad — a role I cherished — but my son, Nick, was well into his twenties and being "dad" now was more like being a good and faithful pal, not the dad who taught him how to throw a baseball, took him camping, showed him how to knot a tie, and saved enough money to send him to a good college.

Perhaps like a lot of men born in the early days of the baby boom, I was staring down the last decades of my life and discovering that the roles I was proud to have filled — happily married man, successful professional, family provider — didn't apply any longer. They had marked my place in the world, a place I had risen to from a tenement on a dead end street in a New England mill town, and now they were gone.

But that wasn't the end of the roles I was losing. Just before the divorce and the sale of the newspapers, my mother and my younger brother — my only sibling — had died within months of each other. I thought I had weathered those deaths without much lasting damage. But when I was sitting by that lake feeling the darkness inside me, I had found myself dwelling on two visions: My mother collapsed and inert in her bed at our modest home and, only a few months before that, my brother dying of a heart attack while lying in the recliner in my mother's house.

Along with those losses went two more identities — son and brother.

If I was not any of those identities now, if they could simply disappear while I was still here, then they must not be who I really am. They were surface answers to the questions: Who am I now? Where do I belong? What am I supposed to do with my life?

Stripped of all my titles, what was left? All those roles I played — as meaningful and gratifying as they were at the time — had they also been substitutes for a deeper self-awareness?

Somewhere in my twenties, as I set about making the life that had provided most of those identities, I had nearly buried my memories of the people and events of my earlier years. They were like a once-beloved book that I believed I had outgrown.

But the feeling of disloyalty I experienced so unexpectedly at the camp in Ontario told me that that book still had something to teach me. Something that the bereft man staring into the Canadian forest and faced with a reasonable request from the woman he wanted to spend the rest of his life with needed to know. I felt I had no choice but to go all the way back to my beginnings to get some answers.

When I was in college I passed almost every day under the hoary quote from Socrates that was carved into the entrance of the library: "Know thyself and thy self will be free."

The only way to do that was the only way I knew how to find out anything. I had spent a good part of my newspaper career writing and editing investigative stories. Now, I had the hardest assignment yet: Investigate myself. Find the threads to my history, and the history to that history, and write about it. A good investigative reporter keeps asking "Why?" until he gets to the why of the why of the why.

It was a daunting challenge and one I doubted I could meet, but I wanted to try. If there was time enough. With my 70th birthday looming, my family medical history suggested I'd better get a move on.

I am the surviving son of a man who died of heart disease in his mid-fifties and the brother of a man who died of a heart problem when he was only fifty. I had the advantage of much better health care and pharmaceuticals than my father had access to in the 1960s, and I had not lived my life as a drug, alcohol and food addict as Gary had. Still, the only two males in my immediate family had died prematurely of heart problems.

Maybe I didn't have a lot more time to answer the questions that age and circumstance had thrust upon me.

Returning to my beginnings meant going back to that tenement on that dead end street, and to my memories not just of my mother and father but of the woman who lived next door to us, a woman who would hold me in her lap and sing to me in her immigrant accent, a woman with the darkest, dampest eyes. I didn't know her story very well, but I knew this much about the woman I called Nana: She carried with her the memory of a murder in an ancient land and the horror of a word forever associated with her identity as an Armenian: genocide. And if I allowed myself to think about it at all, it seemed to me that my childhood had been lived under the shadow of that long ago atrocity.

So maybe the way to start looking for answers about myself was to find out what had happened to her. If I could understand how it might have affected her, then I might also understand the impact it had had on those who followed — including me.

Nana on the steps of her tenement on Wentworth Street,
Dover, N.H. Date unknown.

CHAPTER 2

The Tammy tape

Somewhere in the 1970s, Americans discovered and reveled in ethnic pride. The melting pot of immigrants who transcended their origins to become full-blooded Americans was replaced by the salad bowl, with its multitude of discrete, individualized ethnicities.

America was the bowl into which all these hyphenated citizens had been tossed. There were Irish-Americans, Greek-Americans, Italian-Americans, German-Americans, Chinese-Americans and many other hyphenates in the mix. The new order held that they could — and should — display pride in their differences, and that they should be able to do so without enduring any prejudice. Or that was the theory, anyway — and the hope.

The Irish and Italians and Puerto Ricans each marched proudly on their special days down the streets of the country's major cities. Ethnic food became and still is the rage. Your family's country of origin — once something you spoke little of, if at all — became the subject of friendly conversation, even boasting.

But for the immigrants from the late 19th to the early 20th century — immigrants like my Armenian grandmother — the past was not something to celebrate. All they wanted to be was American and the same went for their hopes for their children, those first-generation Americans.

While Nana did hang on to the food from her past, at least for Sunday dinners and for holidays when she made dishes like stuffed grape leaves and shish kebab, she also worked hard at learning how to "cook like an American" — pork chops, hamburgers, mashed potatoes and, especially, desserts. Her lemon meringue pie could have won a prize at a county fair.

Her American-ness was something she treasured. The love she felt for her new country was not to be questioned. On her meager income she bought World War II savings bonds. And she passed her patriotism down to her children. All of Nana's boys served in the military. As for my mother — even in her retirement she volunteered at her local polling place, and each year she bought a new patriotic decoration for her Christmas tree.

My parents — both of them born to immigrants — also strived to be part of the melting pot and they wanted the same — even more so — for their kids.

However, their steadfast commitment to being Americans, no hyphen wanted, turned out to be an obstacle to getting the story of their history, and mine.

As an investigative reporter, one of the first places you go looking for the truth is to the witnesses. Nana had been dead for more than 20 years by the time I went on my search, and my mother and two of her siblings were also gone. Though two aunts and an uncle were still alive, and I hoped I could get details from them, they didn't have anywhere near the full story of what had happened to their mother in that faraway ancient land, the Ottoman Empire, more than 100 years ago. Nor did they seem much interested in finding out.

They hadn't rejected the past, but they had been raised to be Americans. This meant not dwelling in the past, not trying to relive the events of a tragic story.

One knew the name of Nana's village.

One had Nana's passport photo from 1921.

One had a few stories about what it was like for Nana when she came to America and about the shabby apartment she shared with her new husband.

I suspected they knew much more, but the more I asked my reporter-like questions, the more I felt like I was prying, forcing them to revisit stories they didn't want to remember or recount.

A probing question might just as well be met with, "Have one of these

9

maple squares, Johnny. You always loved them."

My aunts did have a suggestion, though: "Get a copy of the tape cousin Tammy made."

Aunt Mary didn't have one, neither did Aunt Lil, but they knew about it. As for me, I didn't even know I had a cousin Tammy, and they didn't know how to find her. But sometime in the past this mysterious cousin had made a tape recording of Nana, and maybe it contained answers to my questions.

Okay, I thought at the time, I'll keep looking for this tape. But as far as I knew, cousin Tammy was not a journalist, not an historian nor a scholar. She might have made the tape when she was just a high school kid working on a school paper assignment. How good could this recording be?

But I had more holes than facts in the snippets of Nana's story. Whatever was on that tape, it might be more than I had so far.

"Cousin Tammy and her tape" was a phrase I learned to hear not as five ordinary words but as a magical concept: the holy grail, the key to a locked box. Or, alternately, just the garbled ramblings of an old lady.

I didn't even know where to find this literally long-lost cousin.

"I think she lives in New Hampshire," said one aunt.

"She used to live in Nashville," said the other.

I kept asking around, emailing, calling, until finally Aunt Nancy, an aunt-by-marriage to my mother's brother Joe, told me very matter-of-factly, as if I should have known this all along, that she had a copy.

A few days later, a package arrived from Myrtle Beach, N. C., where Joe and Nancy spend the winters, and out slipped, not a tape, but a CD inside a clear jewel case, marked in bold black letters, "NANA 1990 INTERVIEW."

Eager as I was to listen to it, I waited a few days until I had a long car trip planned and could play it in the solitude of the car. As I headed south from central Maine to see friends in Massachusetts in the spring of 2015, I slipped the off-white disc into the Suburu's CD player.

First, a young, American voice, asking: "You were born in 1899?"

Then, a voice I had not heard in more than 20 years, a tender voice, the voice that sang me a German rhyme while I was bounced on her knee, the voice of an immigrant: a slight accent, I surmised later, picked up from the German Lutheran nuns who cared for her at an orphanage in Beirut. A voice that spoke English words, but with the syntax of a woman who was raised speaking other languages — Armenian, Turkish, German.

"Eighteen nine-ta-nine. At least dat's what they, my muth-ah, would have given us."

Listening to that voice, I could just picture my Nana — Gulenia "Rose" Hovsepian Banaian — sitting in her rocking chair in her tiny subsidized apartment in Dover as she spoke into the tape recorder those first words of her life story.

In my mind's eye I could see one of the afghans she was always knitting — probably the blue-and-red one with the scalloped hem — draped over the sofa while her great niece Tammy sat at her feet, asking questions, running the tape recorder. And I could hear my mother and Nana's son Licky, who lived with Nana in the apartment, interrupting with shouted comments whenever they thought their mother had left out an essential part of the story. They were probably sitting at the kitchen table, one room away, drinking coffee and smoking while listening in on Tammy and Nana.

"Ma," said Licky, in his hoarse cigarette-and-coffee voice. "Don't forget to tell her about General Foch." (Nana, who had worked as a chambermaid for the American consul in Beirut, had once greeted the French general at the door — a story Licky loved to hear recounted.)

"Yeah, yeah. That comes after, Steph-an" she said to Licky, her youngest son; she was the only one to call him by his given name, Stephen, but pronounced as it would be in her native language.

My mother, in an even deeper cigarette-and-coffee voice, corrected Nana when she strayed from the sequence of her story.

"You told her you docked at Ellis Island, so go from Ellis Island."

Nana, irritated, replied, "I'm coming to dat."

Mispronunciations. Wrong prepositions. Verbs missing or in the wrong tense. Sentence fragments. It is the voice I grew up with, its phrasing and accent revealing that she had come from another land, its sometimes-mournful tone revealing that she hadn't been safe there, that she had endured great losses. But I had also sensed in that voice — confirmed by the stories I heard her speaking into the tape recorder — a confidence in the present, an assurance that she had accomplished great things against all odds and that all was now well.

Hearing her evoked in me a memory beyond the usual scenes from the past we all recall when triggered by a smell or a taste or a sound from the past. This was a memory of an emotion: There was never a time, from my earliest years to the last time I saw Nana, that I did not want to be in her presence, did not want her eyes on me, did not want to give in to her hugs.

When I heard her voice, I was no longer a man in his sixties, a man with responsibilities and worries. No — just for those moments I was all the endearing names she had ever called me: Johnny, John Quincy Adams, Professor Shingle-dingle. It didn't matter what she was saying. What transported me was hearing that voice. For that moment she was alive again, living next door, slipping shish kebab off a skewer and onto my plate.

But when I came out of my reverie, had recovered from the wave of emotion I felt, I played the recording again and this time focused on the story. It wasn't always told sequentially. There were many holes, some of which could have been filled by asking the right question. But the interview went a long way towards answering the mystery of what had happened to Nana — and what had happened to her children, and her grandchildren, as a result.

As Nana said on the tape, "It's a sad life."

The Ottoman Empire, 1900.

CHAPTER 3

"They're killing the kefir"

When Nana speaks into the tape recorder, the year is 1990 and she is 91 years old. But her heart travels back to 1909, to a spring day in Suedia, a Turkish village close enough to the Mediterranean that on that day it is likely that a sea breeze ruffled the mulberry trees that grew everywhere on the hills. Her mother had sent her to move the family's cows to a field where a shepherd was to watch over them.

"I was barefooted and getting them out of the stall and chase them down the garden to the brook — and I almost see the brook now — and they went grazing, and I was coming back to the mulberry trees and the mulberry leaves were tapping my face and I was running and I was a kid and hadn't eaten yet, nothing.

"A boy, a Turkish boy, hollers to me. I never forget it, never could forget it. In Turkish he said, 'They're killing the kefir.' You know, they call us kefir. You know what it means? Well, it's bad word. They want to talk about the Armenians, they say, 'the kefir, unbelievers'."

The Turkish boy was talking about Gulenia and her family, the Hovsepians, and about all the other Armenians in Suedia, Christians who were living in the Ottoman Empire, which was ruled by Muslims. The news of what that Turkish boy said to Gulenia — "They're killing the infidels" — had reached her parents while she was in the pasture. When she raced home, arriving breathless, there was her father, Elias Hovsepian, heading out the door carrying a rifle, a pistol and a sabre.

The Ottoman Empire's nascent hatred and suspicion of the Christian Armenians had once again turned to violence. Elias was likely on his way to join with other Armenians to defend themselves from what was soon to be known worldwide as the massacre of Adana, the large Turkish city where the pogrom that stretched into the villages such as the Hovsepians' had begun.

"He hugged me, he kissed me, but he didn't say nuthin'," Nana — Gulenia — recalled on the recording.

Her father ran towards a hill on his way to a brook that he intended to follow into the village square.

"But before he gets there, on the hill ..." and then she just stopped speaking, and I imagine her head bowed as she went back into her deepest memories to relive what happened next.

"All I'll say is, hundreds of them."

And then, bluntly: "He was killed. He was beaten."

His body was found near the brook, not far from their farmhouse.

"He couldn't fight all those people. He tried, he did. They had taken everything off him, only his white shirt, homespun white shirt that goes way down to the knee. It's all homespun, rough stuff, and left him there. Left him there."

Exactly how he was killed is uncertain. Sometimes Nana says beaten, other times killed by a sword. However, the most common means of murder of Armenians in the villages was by a tool kept in every rural home: an ax.

As she told that story in her tidy apartment, her stockings would have been rolled up to just below her knees, her ever-present flowered apron draped in her lap. But in her heart, that spring day was not 80 years ago. It was now, and she still felt those mulberry leaves tickling her cheeks as she ran home to a life that was about to change irrevocably.

• • •

"Turkish rule meant unutterable contempt ...
The Armenians were dogs and pigs to be spat upon."
— British ethnographer William Ramsey, 1897

Nana's parents, Elias and Miriam, made their living as farmers and by selling the leaves from their mulberry trees as food for silk worms. They had five children: Gulenia, who was to become my grandmother, was ten years old when the Turks came for the Armenians; Sarah, twelve, Joseph, six, Violet, five, and Moses, not quite a year old and not walking yet.

After the murder of their husband and father, the Hovsepians had no time to mourn. Now, alone in the farmhouse they rented from a Turkish man, Gulenia's mother Miriam had to protect herself and her five children, none of them old enough to be of much help to her in such dire straits.

Now, on that spring day in 1909, they were no longer villagers, no longer farmers, no longer a happy family.

Now they were prey.

Prey for the raging Turks who had killed Elias Hovsepian and left his body, stripped of all but a homespun shirt, on that rocky slope near a brook that fed the Orontes River.

Prey for what was called at the time "one of the most gruesome and savage bloodbaths recorded in human history" — though it was but a prelude for what was to come.

The bloodbath had begun just days before in the city of Adana, 150 miles away from the Hovsepians' village. It's unlikely that they or the other Armenians in the village knew what was happening in Adana, or were aware that the violence in Adana was coming their way. There was no system of getting news — no local newspaper, no radio, no telephone. There was just a town crier, and his job was to stand in a central location and announce only the "news" that came from Ottoman officials.

He was not going to give advance notice of what was the official Ottoman position: The Armenians — the infidels, the Christians, the "kefir" — had to be put in their place.

There is no more ancient Christian people than the Armenians. Armenia declared itself an official Christian nation in the 4th century — the first sovereignty to do so. In the time of the Hovsepians, though, there was no nation of Armenia. There had once been an Armenian nation — two of them in fact: western Armenia, in what is now Turkey, and eastern Armenia, closer to the Turkish-Iranian border. But western Armenia was conquered by the Ottomans in the 16th century, eastern Armenia by Russians in the 19th century.

So, the Hovsepians and the millions of other Armenians in the Ottoman Empire were a people without a country. At the time, the empire established by Turkey in the 14th century included what are now the countries of Turkey, Hungary, Yugoslavia, Greece, Romania, Syria, Iraq, Lebanon, Israel, Jordan and a small section of Russia on Turkey's eastern border — a population of more than 15 million.

The Armenians and other Christians under Ottoman Empire rule lived as second-class citizens under a ruthless Islamic regime that saw them as "the other," a dangerous other to be oppressed and exploited. Armenians paid taxes that were double those paid by the Muslim population. The Kurds within the empire, most of them Muslim, were allowed to extort Armenians and kill those who did not comply without penalty because infidels deserved no protection. Armenians were denied standing in the Ottoman court system — which effectively meant an Armenian could not sue a Muslim or be a witness. There was no punishment for the rape and abduction of Armenian women by Turks or Kurds; and officials were allowed to confiscate Armenian boys for conversion to Islam and forced military service.

There was one additional –and classic — way to keep a resentful and oppressed minority under control: Forbid them to own weapons. However, like repressed minorities throughout history, they sometimes found ways to obtain and hide those weapons, as Gulenia's father had done — for all the good it did him when he confronted his murderers on that rocky hillside.

The humiliation of Armenians was also an everyday fact of life under Ottoman rule. Armenians had to be deferential to Muslims in public; they could be punished for riding a horse when a Muslim was passing by: they had to wear clothes that made them easily identifiable as not Muslim.

This was similar to the way Nazi Germany would treat the Jews just a few decades later. Just as the Turks depicted Christians as a despicable "other," Nazi propaganda depicted Jews as dogs and vermin. The Nazis also required Jews to wear a Star of David patch to make them easily identifiable; they also limited Jews' legal rights; and after 1938, they also prohibited Jews from owning any form of weapon, even a knife.

In the early years of the 20th century, 50 years before the Nazis would kill millions of Jews in gas chambers to solve the "Jewish question," Ottoman Turkey under Sultan Abdul Hamid II, the so-called "Bloody Sultan," was grappling with "the Armenian question." What should the empire do with those millions in their midst they did not trust because they were infidels? Such questions tend to arise in times of chaos and change. Armenians were a "problem" in that era because Turkey was losing its empire and needed a scapegoat, just as the Jews would be the scapegoat Hitler would use to explain Germany's post-World War I ills. German Jews, like many Armenians, were successful and educated in numbers disproportionate to their share of the population, so it was easy to inflame public opinion against them.

By the time Gulenia was born in 1899, Armenian hopes of better treatment under Ottoman rule had been raised and dashed a number of times. Attempts by the European powers to force the Ottoman empire to improve treatment of its Christian minorities had backfired. Sultan Abdul Hamid ignored the Great Powers; their interfering made him more resentful and vengeful towards the Armenians. The few encouraging signs of tolerance turned out to be the sort of lies evil makes to lull its victims while it sharpens the knife. In the 1890s, the "Bloody Sultan" had 300,000 Armenians killed in a series of pogroms.

Armenians were not docile; they tried to fight back, just as Gulenia's father had gathered his weapons when he heard the Turks were coming for the infidels. But the strength and the cruelty of the Ottomans were too much for the outnumbered Armenians.

In one village, for example, Armenians tried to resist, but as they were being beaten they realized they were no match for the Turkish army. The Turkish commander said he would free the Armenian rebels — who were led by a local priest — if they surrendered peacefully. But as soon as they gave up their arms, the commander had the priest seized and his eyes gouged out. Then, they bayoneted him to death. The women of the village were separated from the men and raped. The next night the men were killed by bayonet within hearing of their wives, sisters and children.

This was the world into which Gulenia Hovsepian was born.

In April 1909 — the same month Gulenia heard those frightening words from the Turkish boy — the Ottoman Empire was in turmoil again. The nationalist, secular movement headed by the Young Turks had deposed the "Bloody Sultan," but their actions inflamed the religious fundamentalists, who demanded implementation of Sharia, the sacred law of the Quran. In Constantinople, a coalition of mullahs, divinity students, dervishes (the Sufi Muslims known for their ecstatic dancing) and renegade soldiers took to the streets, sacking and looting government offices.

Word about the uprising spread across the country and resonated in Adana, the home province of the Hovsepians, which was once the center of the ancient Armenian state called Cilicia. Tensions were especially high there: Poorer Turks resented the successful Armenians who lived in the city, although the rural Armenians in the region, like my family, were struggling farmers and shepherds. The attitude of the Armenians in Adana was a factor, too. Hopeful that their condition might improve with the recent deposing of the sultan, they were emboldened to agitate for their rights. They were getting "pushy"– the word the majority always throws at a minority to keep them in their place.

Exactly how the massacre began is lost in the passage of time and the chaos of any spontaneous event. But in the second week of April, foreign diplomats in the city reported seeing dead Armenians in the streets of Adana and Turks roaming Armenian neighborhoods carrying clubs and revolvers.

In the first 48 hours of the massacre, civilian Turks and local police killed 2,000 Armenians and set Armenian homes and businesses on fire. The new government sent in the army, ostensibly to stop the killing. But, instead, the army — falsely claiming that it was fired on by Armenians — entered the Christian quarter of the city and opened fire.

Total death count from the Adana massacre: 15,000 to 25,000 Armenians.

It was yet another incident in the continuum of cruelty to the Armenians, a continuum that went back to the 1880s and forward to 1915, the year Turkey finally solved its "Armenian Question" by killing 1.5 million Armenians. The systematic murder of the Armenians in 1915 was the event that inspired the coining of the word genocide by the legal scholar Raphael Lemkin. It combines the Greek word for family or race — genos — and the Latin word "cide," meaning killing.

In the weeks after Adana's Armenian neighborhoods were destroyed, the killing spread to the smaller cities and the small towns, as far away as that little village on the Mediterranean where the Hovsepians tended their cows and sheep and made a modest living harvesting the leaves of the mulberry tree.

In one day, all of that was in the past. Now, Miriam — an uneducated peasant woman around 30 years old — had to save herself and her family. Should she flee, stay put, go into hiding? She didn't know what to do, so she went where anyone would go back then: to the only authority in the village, a man Nana referred to as the mayor of Suedia. He was probably a Turkish official.

Miriam and her children weren't the only ones in the village fearful and confused — when they reached the mayor's home, they found that many of the other villagers were already gathered in a large upstairs room.

Nana remembered, "They were all sitting there, and we all climbed — it was on the second floor — and they were all sitting around and my mother had the baby in her arms and my mother was mad, real mad" — at their Turkish landlord, who was there, too.

"He used to come to the house, used to eat with my father," Nana recounted. And her mother said to him, "You put your hands in the plate as Elias had put his hands. How could you do anything like that to him?"

The landlord replied, "Well, I couldn't do nothing about it."

"My mother let him have it," Nana said, using a phrase she would have picked up probably long after emigrating and likely from her boys.

Miriam was "all worked up," while the Turk was calm and "proper." He told them to stay in their house, and he would send a man to stand guard "so they won't chase, won't hurt us."

But Miriam was suspicious and instead she gathered up her children and walked to the silk factory where they sold their mulberry leaves, a factory Nana said was owned by a North African couple.

The young, recently married couple put the family behind a locked door in a section of the factory "and we heard the soldiers going by because it was on the main road, and Violet started to cry and my mother would put her hand on her mouth so they don't hear it …" Her baby sister was only five years old "and you know how kids are at that age: 'I'm hungry, I'm hungry. I want to eat.'"

Since there was food at home, Miriam told Gulenia to make her way back there, get what she could, and bring it to their secret hideout.

"You climb that wall, you go to our yard," were her mother's words to the ten-year-old.

But when Gulenia got close to home she saw "hundreds of people around our place," so she I ran back to the silk factory and knocked on the door until the couple who was hiding them let her in.

They couldn't stay hidden in the factory indefinitely, however, and something happened — Nana's story had gaps — that forced them out of hiding and into the hands of the Turks.

"They said they were taking us to Antakya (Antioch) and we were supposed to turn Mohammedan. The landlord had made arrangements for us to go to this place and we will turn Mohammedan. Yes, convert."

(Conversion to Islam erased the greatest offense of the Armenians: being Christian infidels. Those who converted were spared. Forced conversion was well-documented at the time, including in dispatches by a German pastor sent to Turkey by his church to record the events of the 1890s massacres and bring aid to the victims. He reported that 15,000 Armenians were forced to become Muslim or face death and that 324 churches had been confiscated and turned into mosques.)

The Hovsepians' Turkish landlord gave them a donkey and their few belongings, wrapped in rags.

"So, all the way we went. Can't tell you how far it was. It couldn't be too far, because we all walked."

Antioch is 18 miles north of Suedia, a longer walk than Nana remembered, and a rocky one in parts. Maybe walking 18 miles back then was not the hardship it would be considered today. Still, it must have been an ordeal for Miriam, caring for five little ones over the four or more days I estimate it would have taken them to make the trip. Where did they sleep? Outside? Or did they find shelter in homes along the way? If they had money, it couldn't have been much — they were farmers and shepherds. Typically, the temperature would have been as cold as 50 degrees at night, rising to the 70s in the daytime.

Nana glossed over this journey on the recording, perhaps because events soon after took a positive turn when they made it to the address their landlord had given them, which was the home of a Muslim woman.

"The woman, the old lady, was very, very nice to us. Very nice." Nana remembered. "I bet if you left it to the women those things wouldn't have happened as bad as they did. See, women didn't amount to nothing then. Woman was nothing but a slave, to cook and have brats. Not now, but those days. That's way back."

I was not surprised to hear Nana speak that way about women, to hear what sounded like modern feminism from a woman who was barely educated, who spent her adult years surviving in a working-class city far removed from these sorts of urban ideas. I was not surprised because I knew that after the early death of her husband she had been both mother and father to her children, both homemaker and provider. She didn't need theories about the second sex to know the strength and power of women, to be both regretful and angry that men were ruining the world while the wisdom of women was ignored.

The Hovsepian family had two relatives living in Antioch, whom Nana referred to as aunts, possibly her mother's sisters, although she never states that directly. They worked for Greeks and lived in the Greek section of the city. Sarah, the oldest sister, had a plan: to ask the Muslim woman if she could visit one of those aunts.

The woman said, "All right, you can go ahead. You know your way, you go ahead."

Miriam understood what was really happening — her oldest daughter was escaping.

Sarah and her mother understood that if she didn't escape she would likely be forced to convert and marry a Muslim man or, if she resisted conversion, be sent to a refugee camp overseen by Turks. The fact that Miriam would risk never seeing her daughter again suggests she knew that was better than letting her fall into the hands of the Turks. After all, these were the people who had just killed her husband. In 1915 they would have no compunction about killing more than a million Armenians through forced deportation and outright murder. Though the official start of that genocide was six years away, the Armenians in Antioch could already feel the hatred of the Turks. It poisoned the very air they breathed.

Fearful of the danger to her 13-year-old daughter, Miriam was prepared to make any sacrifice to spare her. She did what little she could to get her ready for whatever would happen next.

"Left with nothing but the clothes on their backs" is the proverbial way to describe the flight of those who are in desperate straits, but for the Hovsepians in Antioch it was a literal reality. To take with them all of their life's belongings, all they had to do was wear them. And that's exactly what Miriam had Sarah do because, as Nana said, "She knew Sarah wasn't coming back."

When Sarah was about to leave, Gulenia started crying, "Mama, I want to go. I'd like to see my aunt, too."

Miriam put two sets of clothes on little Gulenia, as well. Now, she and Sarah could both escape.

Then Miriam herself started crying, for she, too, wanted to go, but, as Nana explained on the tape, "she couldn't leave the other kids, the baby in her arms and all," and she must have known that the aunt could not take them all in.

Their Muslim keeper — Nana called her "the old lady" — was "very nice about it," Nana remembered: "Go, visit your family," she told them. She even allowed Miriam to accompany the two girls to their aunt's.

But, Nana said, "She had no idea we weren't gonna come back."

Nana didn't say who took care of the three young ones while Miriam was gone, but perhaps it was their kind-hearted host.

Precisely what happened after Miriam returned to the Muslim woman's home is not clear, but eventually she and her three youngest children were sent from there to a refugee camp.

Nana remembered that shortly after she and her sister went to their aunt's house, town criers circulated in the region with an order from the government: "They holler and yell, 'Stop it. Don't kill no more.'"

For the moment the Armenians were safe. But the virulent religious hatred did not go away just because one episode had officially ended. In 1915 it would return with a ferocity that ended in the death more than a million of the two million Armenians living in Turkey at the time and the exile of most of those not killed.

But for Gulenia, a savior was on the way, a man she spoke of all these years later on the recording with awe and affection — her Uncle George.

Illustration of the Adana, Turkey massacre, 1909. Le Petit Journal, Paris, France.

CHAPTER 4

Bread and cucumbers

While the Hovsepians were refugees in Antioch, 500 miles away in Cairo, the foreman at a factory turning out English cigarettes had some somber news for George Yusef Antaki, one of his workers.

"I heard that your brother has been killed," he said.

George's brother was Elias Hovsepian, Nana's father. George had dropped his Armenian surname and taken the more Muslim-sounding name to stay clear of trouble while he was living in Egypt, another Islamic country.

When George heard that his brother was dead and the Hovsepians had been forced to leave their home, Nana said he "took off" to find them. He had enough cash from gambling winnings — "50 Turkish pounds, and that's a lot of money in those days," Nana says on the recording — to book a ticket on a ship out of Cairo. He sailed to the Turkish port city of Iskendrum, known historically as Alexandretta, which was just up the Mediterranean coast from Suedia.

From the way Nana remembered him, George Antaki seems to have been the prototypical bachelor uncle: He liked to gamble, he liked to travel, and he liked to spoil his nieces and nephews.

Nana remembered him visiting in Suedia: "I always thought a lot of him. I'd say, 'Uncle, uncle' all the time. He used to send us things, you know … clothes and all that."

Decades later, I too would have such an uncle — Nana's youngest son, my Uncle Licky.

Even though the killings had been called off, George was still in fear as he traveled to the Ottoman Empire.

"He was afraid," Nana said, "because you can tell he was Armenian with the features and all. He was afraid they might kill him, too."

But George had a protector with him, a talisman.

"He had been to the United States, see, and he had a flag, a little flag pin sticking in his suit … and they see that flag, they don't touch him. You're an American."

(Later, when he returned to Cairo and the local authorities were rounding up Armenians because there had been a threat on the life of a visiting Ottoman official, the land of the brave saved George again. When the police came to George's apartment building, he hung an American flag out the window. "When they see the flag, forget it," Nana said. "They wouldn't touch him.")

By the time George arrived, Gulenia had been taken in by an Antioch family as their maid, an arrangement that appears to have been made by the aunt that she and Sarah had escaped to, although that is never clear from the recording. One day, she answered a knock on the door, and there — much to her surprise — was her uncle.

He must have known where to find her because of a family connection between himself and Gulenia's aunt in Antioch, although that connection is never explained on the recording. The sight of her beloved uncle was too much for Gulenia.

"I cried something awful. They couldn't stop me from crying, and I put my arms up and he say to me, 'Go get your stuff. I'm taking you. I'm going to send you to school.' When I heard that, I was in heaven. I wanted always to go to school," she said, her voice on the recording filled with the pain she still felt at the memory of that long-ago desire.

Her brother Joseph had been sent to school when they lived in Suedia, and, as she remembered, time and again she would ask her father, "Papa, why can't I go?" He'd say, 'Girls don't go to school.' That's true. Girls got married and had kids. That's it." But Gulenia always wanted more for herself. Later in that same recording she talked about a cousin offering her an arranged marriage. She was in her late teens then, with few options, and another girl might have said yes. Not Gulenia. Her response shows her independent streak and the ambition that had not yet been knocked out of her by hard times:

"They were going to marry me off to someone who makes wooden spoons. Oh, that's funny, you know!" she said, amused at the very thought, even at the age of 92 as she looked back on that moment. "I was thinking big," she said. "My mind was different."

George explained to the family Gulenia was working for that he wanted to take his niece away to a place that would be better for her than Turkey.

Working with a missionary, George was gathering a group of Armenian refugee children who were to be sent to an orphanage for girls in Beirut. Although Nana didn't say, the missionary was probably from Germany, because the orphanage was a German-run Lutheran institution. Beirut was far enough away from the Adana district to be considered safe, even though Lebanon at the time was also under the power of the Ottomans; it was safer yet because the children would be in the care of an institution associated with a strong foreign power.

The plan was to choose 45 Armenian girls, no more than two from each family. Some of the girls, like Gulenia, were living in local homes; others were in refugee camps.

But who was to go with Uncle George and Gulenia? Older sister Sarah or younger sister Violet? Sarah was 13, and Nana recalled that Sarah could easily have been lost to the family during the recent massacre because she was young and female. But Sarah "was lucky — they didn't take her. You know, the Turks didn't take her. Because they took all those girls. They used them." Nana doesn't elaborate but the meaning is clear, backed up by the historical records, which document some of the cruelest atrocities inflicted on women and girls during the pogroms: rape, forced prostitution or sale to a harem.

Having decided that Sarah was now safe, Miriam chose to send little Violet, who was then only six years old, with Uncle George and Gulenia.

"That night, my mother gave us a bath and cleaned the lice out of our hair. Everything she could, clean clothes … comb my hair … and she took a little piece of cloth and put in there cucumbers and some kind of bread they make … a lot of sesame seeds on it. She put that in there for the two of us to eat ... and we all gathered. They had to take us in the dark to the missionary. It was midnight."

Their next stop was the ancient city of Iskenderun, the former Alexandretta, which had been founded 330 years before the birth of Christ by its namesake, Alexander the Great. From there they were to board a ship to Beirut. Although the Adana massacre had been officially called off, this was still dangerous territory for a large group of vulnerable children whose appearance could easily give them away as "the other." Perhaps the Sultan's rescission order had not been heard everywhere. Perhaps some Turks were still angry over the Adana massacre, where Armenians had fought back and killed many of their countrymen.

Nana never explained how the missionary and Uncle George got the 45 girls to Iskenderun, but she did remember that when they got there they were put into an empty building and given a meal of a mysterious substance.

"One of the girls, wise girl, says, 'You know what you eatin'? You eatin' worms ... They just boil some worms and that's what they're feeding us.'"

Hungry as she must have been, her disgust was more powerful still, and you can hear it on the recording: "I NEVER touch mine. I would not touch it. I would not let my little sister touch it either"

Many years later, she was fed a similar meal on the ship to America and by then she knew what it was: spaghetti.

What Nana's recorded recollection lacked in continuity, it made up for in details, especially when it came to food. An 18-mile forced hike from her village to Antioch is tossed off in a few words, but she remembered every detail of some of the meals, even one she refused to eat, or, in another case, food that she only heard about — something offered to her sisters in the refugee camp while she was working as a maid:

"I went to the camp and visited my mother and kids. My sisters and all. They had given them some chocolates ... and my little sister ... she took the candy, threw them in the cistern. She didn't know what it was. She thought it was turd or something. I wouldn't know it either. We never saw chocolates."

Food was never a topic with my Irish father or his family (I don't recall ever being given anything to eat at his mother's house except hard candy or a Coke), but on my mother's side food — like the stuffed grape leaves, pilaf and flat bread Nana prepared — was the center around which daily life revolved.

This is typical of many ethnic immigrant homes, where foods from home bring back memories of the places they have left. But there was an added dimension, I believe, to the importance of food for a woman who had a history of not enough. Beginning on the day her family was driven from her village until well into her life in America, Nana often had cause to worry about where her next meal would come from.

Would her mother be able to scrape up bits of bread and cucumbers for her? Would the German missionary — a stranger — provide, and would it be food she could even recognize? Once she got to the Beirut orphanage she was dependent upon the goodwill of the nuns for her food. Even after she came to America, my aunts told me, she was sometimes ill from hunger either because she didn't have enough money or because she didn't know what food to buy or how to prepare it.

Aunt Mary, Nana's middle daughter, recalls her mother telling her that when she first joined her new husband in Dover where he was working in the mills, they bought only the cheapest food so they could "save every penny … because they were going back to the old country." But they never went — even after the Turks were defeated in World War I, the new government in Turkey was still killing Armenians.

As a young bride in America, my Aunt Mary said, Nana "was very set on learning how to cook. She would meet someone, and they would tell her they made this or that and she would ask, 'How did you do it?'"

By the time I came around, Nana had survived two world wars, the Depression, the death of her husband just after their youngest was born, and more deprivations than I will ever know about. But along the way she had become a master of American cooking: Toll House cookies, lemon meringue pie, apple pie, roast chicken, pork chops, chicken-and-rice soup.

"Johnny, you vant somedin' ta eat?" she'd ask me, whether I was five years old and visiting her after school, or fifty when I would come to her little apartment with my wife and son. I would never say no because whatever she made — chicken soup, stuffed grape leaves, even a hamburger — was the best you ever had. The soup made you feel restored; the grape leaves melted in your mouth and released that musty taste of lamb; and why was the lowly hamburger so good in her kitchen, both crusty and tender? Even the ketchup seemed better in Nana's kitchen.

I didn't know it when I was a boy, but I came to know later why everything Nana made tasted so wonderful. It was because she made all of it with her own hands — her hands chopping onions, her hands rolling the grape leaves, her hands forming the hamburger. Hands that held my face up to her face, a face now turned from sadness to joy. A joy that I came to understand she had waited for since she was that girl with the cucumbers and sesame bread Miriam had wrapped in a cloth.

It was the last meal she would ever be fed by her mother.

Armenian woman kneeling beside dead child in field near Aleppo, Syria (part of Ottoman Empire) during the genocide. Photo in public domain.

CHAPTER 5

"Gonna burn us to death"

Somewhere in Iskenderun, 45 little Armenian girls huddled together in the empty building they'd been taken to for their last night in Turkey. Safety was just a day away, for when they awoke in the morning, their ship would be waiting to take them to Beirut and the orphanage.

As they lay sleeping, Nana recalled, the missionaries woke them, yelling, "Get your bundle!" and had them run as fast as they could to a building closer to the port.

Later, the adults told Nana and the other children why they had had to leave in such a panic:

Turks had discovered the children were hiding and about to escape and were coming with cans filled with kerosene.

"They were going to light it up and the whole place go on fire. Someone found out about it so they had to take us. They were gonna burn us all to death."

Her story fits the facts of the period. Setting fire to a building full of infidels was just one of the killing methods employed by the Turks and their surrogates, the Kurds, from the time of the Adana massacre in 1909 to the genocide six years later. These fires were documented by a variety of sources, including American and European officials and missionaries in Turkey at the time.

In 1915, for example, in an Armenian farming region, Turkish police and Kurdish killing squads together murdered most of the men of the region and then herded the elderly, women and children into a barn where they were "packed like sardines," according to a boy who escaped. Then, they set the barn on fire.

Other methods employed to kill Armenians: poisoning wells with offal; death by starvation or thirst during forced marches through the desert; driving Armenians off cliffs into rivers where they would drown; and death by repeated rape. To save ammunition, children were lined up in a row and dispatched with one bullet. Soldiers on horseback would gallop down a line of women and slice off heads.

But Gulenia was lucky again. Lucky to have made it out of Suedia. Lucky to have avoided forced conversion. Lucky that Uncle George was himself lucky at the gambling tables.

Lucky now to escape being burned alive.

The orphanage in Beirut was run by German Lutheran nuns — which explains Nana's German-accented English. (When I was listening to the recording of her recollections, I realized that she sounded like someone else, like someone whose accent I had become familiar with as a fan of Jewish humor: She sounded just like Mel Brooks' 2,000-year-old man.)

She seems to have been happy and safe at the orphanage, recalling that the nuns allowed the Armenians to go to their own Armenian Apostolic Church on holidays and didn't ask them to convert to Lutheranism. She especially liked going to a classroom every day and learning, loved it so much that her diploma from the Zoar Orphan and Education House came all the way with her from Beirut to Cairo, across the Atlantic to Ellis Island and, finally, to Dover. It survives still, framed and hanging in the California home of Nana's youngest daughter, Lillian.

On the tape Nana recounts many anecdotes from her life during her time in Beirut. Once she turned sixteen, she was too old to remain in the orphanage, so the nuns there found her a job at the American consulate in Beirut. The three years Gulenia spent working as a chambermaid at the consulate, making beds, cleaning up and greeting visitors, provided some of the most vivid memories she would recount on Tammy's tape some 70 years later.

I'd heard some of those stories even before I heard the tape, including the one about her encounter with General Ferdinand Foch, the supreme allied commander, a story her son Licky, who was a veteran and admired all things military, had always been impressed by and often asked her to recount.

It was not long after World War I had ended, during the period when the victorious French occupied Beirut, that she opened the consulate door to discover that it was General Foch who had come to call. He deposited his calling card on the silver tray she held out to him. It was in the late morning, and the consul, who had a habit of staying up late and sleeping late, had to be roused. While he got dressed, Gulenia, the teenage chambermaid, showed the general and his two guards to the consulate's cavernous salon.

"… The room as big as this building, walled, thirteen cupboards, marble floor, Persian carpets, even the chapel was in there," she remembered. "And the lights used to fascinate me. Every light bulb was a different color. When that would go on, I used to go crazy 'cause we had, (at) school only … one light, sticking out ceiling. Right, General Foch, that's how I met him, very short man, short and stocky. Something like Napoleon."

Two days later the general returned to the consulate, Nana remembers, dressed in his best uniform for a victory ceremony. Crowds had gathered below, soldiers fired a salute and cheers of "Vive la France!" rose from the street. The Allies had defeated Germany and the rest of the Central Powers, including the Ottoman Empire. This meant that the Ottoman Empire was no longer an empire, and those who had persecuted the Armenians were out of power.

On the tape Nana also relates the little news she had of family back home during her time in Beirut. While still at the orphanage she heard that her little brother Moses was living with her sister Sarah and Sarah's husband, who was a Turk and a soldier in the Ottoman army. (Whether this was a forced marriage, or a marriage Sarah chose to save herself, or a marriage between two people who actually loved each other is unknown. Nana never explains in the recording how this marriage came about, but decades later, in the 1950s, Nana received a letter from Sarah and found out she had left her Turkish husband, moved to the Republic of Armenia and married an Armenian.)

As for what befell her mother after she and Violet left Turkey — that comes up only as an aside when she reflected on the fact that the Turkish government was still denying the genocide that enraged her own family (as it continues to do to this day).

31

"It happened," she said, in a rare defiant tone. "My father went. My brother starved to death … my mother died on the road."

"How did that happen?" my cousin asked her on the tape, but Nana had no clear answer. She didn't find out about her mother's death until January 1916, when she received a letter from her sister Violet. Although the two girls were both in Beirut, they were communicating by letter because Gulenia's job at the American consulate was in a different part of town from the orphanage where Violet, being younger, was still living.

Where Miriam lived in the years between her daughters' departure from Turkey and her own death is one of the many gaps in the story of the Hovsepians. She probably had to leave the refugee camp where Gulenia had said goodbye to her and at some point, as the war was spreading throughout the Ottoman lands, she must have fallen into the hands of the Turks. The timing of the letter from Violet suggests that Miriam died in late 1915, height of the genocide.

Nana's assertion that her mother died on the road makes sense in that context, because death "on the road" was the primary way the Turks killed the Armenians during the genocide. They marched hundreds of thousands of Armenians to detention camps. Those who did not die on the road by exposure or, if they lagged, by shooting, beating or stabbing, were killed at one of the camps or died from disease or starvation.

If Nana was depressed or bitter or defeated by these losses, it was not obvious to me when I was growing up. She was always so warm and gentle with her eight grandchildren that we had little sense of her suffering. When it came to taking care of us, nothing could break her good humor.

The pain must always have been there, but I only discovered its depth when I listened to Tammy's tape and heard her tell the story of what happened to her baby brother, Moses.

Armenian women, children and elderly men deported from their homes during the genocide by the Ottoman Turks. Tens of thousands of Armenians died on these forced marches through the Syrian desert. Photo from the Wagner Collection, courtesy of the Armenian National Institute.

CHAPTER 6

A heart in pieces

Nisrine kept teaching school for months as the siege tightened around the Syrian town of Madaya, but had to give up a few weeks ago when her students got too weak from starvation to walk to class. A local medic has been surviving on the rehydration salts he gives patients, while a business school graduate makes soup from grass for his 70-year-old father, consulting shepherds about which kinds their long-since-slaughtered flocks liked best.

— New York Times, Jan. 14, 2016

"… soup from grass …"- the world was shocked at this report from the war in Syria. Under a murderous siege by both the Syrian government and its allies, including the Lebanese militia Hezbollah, the people of Madaya, having eaten every cat and dog in their village, were now eating the last thing they could find to fill the aching emptiness in their stomachs. It would fill them for a moment, but humans cannot digest grass. Instead of nourishing them, it causes diarrhea, which leads to dehydration and even death.

Some things don't change, unfortunately. Madaya is only a few hundred miles from Suedia, the Armenian village in Turkey where Nana was born and where her father was murdered in 1909.

Something else was the same, too.

One hundred years before the world read of the plight of starving Syrians, it was moved so deeply by the starvation of my ancestors that the phrase "the starving Armenians" was commonplace in the West. Mothers remonstrated with their children to finish their dinners in the name of the starving Armenians — starved by genocide and the simultaneous deprivations of the First World War.

As I was doing this research, I came across photo after photo showing the cruelty of the Turks. Pictures of a woman and her two children, dead, naked and starved to the point of being nothing more than skeletons. Armenians hanging in a public square from make-shift gallows. And from the Adana massacre, the event that deprived Nana of her father and sent the Hovsepians into hiding, I found a photo of two Armenian children lying naked, their backsides to the camera to show what had been done to them — their flesh had been ripped off with cotton-chopping tools and their knee tendons severed.

To see those photos and know they are your people makes you want to scream and weep and scream again. To be an Armenian and to see, as I have, photos of naked mothers and children lying dead on their backs, their ribs as prominent as barrel staves, their faces the same dark and pleading eyes as my mother's and grandmother's, made me realize the short distance between the life I have and the lives that got me here.

But for Nana, no photos were necessary to provoke in her the horror I felt when I saw those images.

A horror many times as powerful as my own because it was personal.

A horror that went back more than 70 years before the moment when she poured her memory of it into that tape machine.

A horror set off not by a photo but by a letter sent to her in 1918, by which time she was living in Cairo.

• • •

In that year, Gulenia was 19. The war was just over. With the Turkish leaders who had organized the genocide out of power, it became safe for Armenians who were living in exile to return to Turkey. It would not stay that way for long — within two years of the WWI armistice, the new government of Turkey would try to annihilate the Armenians still in the country. But for that brief window it was safe for Armenians to travel throughout the former Empire, and Gulenia was ready to leave Beirut. Not for Turkey, however.

A distant cousin came to the consulate and offered to help Gulenia return to Suedia. Other displaced Armenians who had survived the genocide were returning with the protection of the French, hoping to reclaim their homes that had been confiscated by Turks.

But Gulenia had no interest in going back. Her parents were dead, and her rescuer, Uncle George, was in Cairo, as was her brother Joseph, who was living with their uncle and whom she hadn't seen in 10 years. That's where she wanted to go, even though her cousin told her it was impossible.

"I said to her, 'I'm walking. I'll walk and go.'"

The cousin knew what she was talking about, however, and when Gulenia went to a refugee camp where officials were issuing papers that would allow Armenians to travel, she ran into trouble. The two officials at the camp sarcastically replied to her plan to go to Egypt: "What we gonna do, hire a special ship just for you."

Furious, she turned on her heel and returned to the consulate where she told her story to the consul. She must have been a good employee, or he was a decent man — or both — because he was incensed at what happened to her and sent her back to the officials, this time accompanied by a guard from the consulate.

"I went with the guard to the window. Everybody waited. I get to the window first. I get my paper to go to Egypt."

Apparently, she had saved enough from her job to get herself to Cairo, where a cousin or a friend from the orphanage — she credits both at different points on the recording — had told her that she could help her get a job as a nurse's aide in a hospital for the British and other Europeans.

Gulenia was not long in Cairo when the fateful letter arrived. It came from someone she identified only as "this woman ... [who] want to make trouble."

The story in the letter is best told in Nana's words, words that leave gaps in the sequence of events, but leave no doubt about what it meant to her then and until her last breath.

"My brother was staying home with my sister, you see, and he didn't have no food. Nothing. He was eating only grass. Grass or anything that grow, you know, you eat vegetable all the time you have the diarrhea, dysentery. And he died, starved to death three weeks before the Armistice was signed. The

Armistice was signed, they had PLENTY, PLENTY FOOD, the Red Cross [here she is near tears]. He was about, 10, 9, 10-years old. He died. I'm never going to forgive anyone for that. Never! Never! It broke my heart, made my heart in pieces.

"When I came to Egypt, we had a letter, you know, told us about it. I cried my eyes out! I cried my eyes out! I said that little boy didn't do nothing. In three weeks he would have lived. But this woman…that write the letter, I think she wanted make trouble. She said, it was him didn't give him the food, Sarah's husband. She said it was him didn't give him no food. But Sarah wrote a letter that said it wasn't that, we just didn't have any. I don't know, I don't want to believe anything. Because war is wartime, see, anything can happen.

"Three weeks after, Armistice started, I said, what happened [now she is weeping]. Plenty food now, all kinds of food coming into the Red Cross. He could have lived. I ain't going to forgive anyone for it [sobbing]. It was bad, bad thing. Sometimes I think about it, lot of times, lot of times, especially when you grow old. Sometimes, you know, I don't know who to forgive, who not."

For Tammy, the cousin who made the recording, this outpouring of emotion came a shock, as it did for me. Gulenia Hovsepian Banaian was a woman who comforted everyone else, who had forearms that could wield the steam iron in a commercial laundry all day, who cooked for everyone, whose house was always neat and clean, whose well of love could not be emptied no matter how many children, grandchildren and great grandchildren dipped their buckets into it. We might cry, but never Nana.

How could Nana have embraced life so fully and with such vigor while being tortured by the images of her baby brother dying of starvation, Tammy wondered.

"No one knows why you are so strong," she said to Nana.

"I don't know why," Nana replied. "Just … He must have something ready for me. I don't know."

And then Nana laughed.

Nana – Gulenia (Rose) Hovsepian —
age approximately 20. Passport photo

CHAPTER 7

From Cairo to America

Having traveled by train and ship, Gulenia arrived in Cairo in May of 1919. She stayed with her uncle and brother, but she says little about Joseph, who is about 15 at this point, except to note that when she got to Cairo he was not there with Uncle George to greet her at the train station — he didn't have the five cents to pay the admission to the station. She also recalled that she didn't see him much afterwards because "he was spending all his time downtown" — likely gambling, it turns out.

In Cairo, she met up with a young woman with whom she had attended the orphanage school who was now working in a hospital for Europeans. Through her, Gulenia got a job there as a nurse's aide.

Gulenia loved the job. It provided her with an income and a private room. Egypt was still a British protectorate and most of the patients at this hospital were English. More than one of the women there offered to take her back to the UK to be a nanny.

But Gulenia turned them down, just as she had refused the offer to marry her off to a maker of wooden spoons and the offer to help her return to Turkey. She had other plans — she wanted to go to America. That opportunity soon presented itself — her friend's aunt had told her about two Armenian brothers living in the U.S. who wanted to marry women from the old country.

Nana recalled that she was told "they're pretty well off. They have money, see … I wasn't only interested in a man … I wanted to see America."

Gulenia went to see the aunt and told her, "I'll think it over." After talking to her friend she decided to go.

The Armenian man Gulenia married in the U.S. was Hovannes Banaian, or, translated, John. He was born in 1889, 10 years before Gulenia, in the city of Malatya, Turkey, where 7,000 Armenians had been killed by Islamic mobs in the 1890s. He came to America in 1909, the same year as the massacre in Adana.

According to family legend, John intended to settle in Portland, Maine, where there was already a substantial Armenian population working in the local mills, but when the train stopped in Dover he got off to stretch his legs. As Nana's daughter Lillian tells it, "sitting there, smoking cigarettes, talking Greek were a bunch of Greeks. So my father got out and says, 'Is there any work here?'" One of the Greeks replied, "Ya, come on."

He said to himself, "To heck with Portland. We'll stay here, the mills are hiring."

(There is a strong affinity between Greeks and Armenians, both Christian minority populations persecuted within the Ottoman Empire.)

At the turn of the century, Dover was a manufacturing juggernaut, turning out millions of feet of cotton and woolen goods, and shoes by the tens of thousands. At the bottom of the mill hierarchy was the tannery, about a block off the city's main street, a place still in operation when I was a boy, spewing its brown, smelly waste into the Cocheco River.

There may be few mill jobs as noxious, as demanding, as exhausting as being a tannery worker. Raw cowhides by the hundreds are stripped, treated with salt, lime and chemicals, dried and turned into leather for belts and shoes. The men who worked there came home stinking of the flesh they had stripped from the hides and splashed with chemicals and toxic water.

That's where Grandfather John Banaian got his first job.

I have a five-by-seven studio portrait of my grandfather. He doesn't look like a struggling factory worker. He's dressed formally in a pinstriped suit, with vest and silk tie and what appear to be pins from fraternal organizations hanging on his lapel. His dark hair is trimmed close to the temples and coiffed in an elegant pompadour. The gaze in those eyes below the high forehead that we share makes a statement — I am determined, I am resolute, I will succeed.

One of my aunts thinks her father must have borrowed the fancy suit, because he didn't have that kind of money, but he had pride and ambition and perhaps wanted to look the part. His plan was to become a landlord and leave the mills behind.

But first, he wanted a wife, a good Armenian woman, and in 1921, the marriage having been arranged in Cairo, he sent Gulenia Hovsepian the money for passage to America. She took a train from Cairo to Alexandria, and on Aug. 9, 1921, at age 21, she crossed the Mediterranean by ship to Piraeus, Greece. A few days later, after seeing the sights in Athens, she took the 550-foot passenger liner King Alexander across the Atlantic to Ellis Island, N.Y.

The food was bad, she said, and she was shocked that the bath water came from the sea. A Greek boy who worked on the ship was "crazy" about her, following her around and slipping her better food. Nana still felt bad all these years later about what happened when the cook found out the boy was stealing food for her — he gave the boy "such a kick in his pants he flew 10 feet."

Three weeks later, the ship docked at Ellis Island, where she waited for 49 days to be processed and allowed to leave.

She and John Banaian were married in a civil service on Ellis Island, then made their way to Dover by train, where they had a proper church marriage.

Gulenia expected to move into a nice home in Dover, but John was not the well-off immigrant she'd been told he was. He lived in a third floor apartment near the tannery with his brother Jacob. The extent of its shabbiness was always expressed in my family with the same anecdote: John Banaian was using dishtowels for window curtains.

On Jan. 10, 1923, about 15 months after they were married, John and Rose Banaian had their first child. Although they themselves were using the American translations of their first names, they gave their daughter a traditional Armenian name — Koharig. "Kohar" means jewel. The "ig" suffix means sweetheart. Later, Koharig gave herself an American middle name — Julia, as in jewel — and adopted an American nickname, Kay.

In the next 10 years, John moved from the awful tannery job to working on an assembly line at a cotton factory, spent his hard-earned savings to buy the three-unit tenement on Wentworth Street into which he moved his family, fathered five more children and, just months after the last one was born, became sick with an ulcer. His wife urged him to slow down because working a full-time job at the factory on top of fixing up the tenement was clearly too much for him. But he didn't, and he contracted double pneumonia. Having escaped a genocide at home, made his way to freedom and safety in the U.S., fed and housed six children through the Great Depression, and worked so hard at his mill jobs that he was able to achieve the American dream of owning a home, he died in April 1933. The tenement he had intended to be the first of his real estate investments turned out to be his last.

Now, his wife — the woman who became my Nana — had to leave her six kids at home and take her husband's job spooling bobbins at the cotton factory. The kids were Koharig, age 10; Elias, known as Dean, nine; Stephen, nickname Licky, seven; George, aka Joe, six; Mary, three; and Lillian, nickname Lity, just two years old.

Until the youngest two were old enough to go to school, the Greek family living in the middle tenement — the one that 40 years later my parents, brother and I would occupy — took care of them while Gulenia was at work.

It fell to Koharig, who was the oldest, to be the backup mother between the time she came home from elementary school until the late afternoon when her mother would finish her shift.

From age 10 until she graduated from high school, Koharig — whose name her brothers and sisters shortened to "Quod" — was the family's caretaker, cook, housekeeper and settler of arguments.

In 2018, I asked my Aunt Mary what she remembered of that time and, in particular, what it meant for that 10-year-old girl — who 15 years after the death of her father would become my mother — to have had to be a substitute mother for her five younger siblings.

Mary said that Koharig had complained to her — "a lot" — about the role that had been thrust upon her. She quoted what I took to be a refrain from her big sister that she had probably heard repeated many times through the years: "I had to take care of you kids!"

"She didn't want to," Aunt Mary said, "I imagine she wanted to play or get out of the house."

As far I know, the chance to play never came for that young girl. The years as big sister on Wentworth Street turned her into a responsible, hard-working young woman, and then into a responsible, hard-working wife and mother, but one with a well of resentment that was never emptied. To use a term of her period, she was a "bossy" woman who demanded a lot of those she loved.

I have her autograph book from her high school graduation. On one of the opening pages, she reveals her personality in a few words:

"Some people are too lazy to write, but I hope you are not one of them."

I said this about her to her friends and family at her wake:

"Thank you all for being here today. I have just one question: Are you here on your own accord, or did Kay order you to be here?"

It was a solemn occasion, but that got a laugh, because her friends, sisters and brothers, all of who loved her for her generosity and loyalty, also knew that side of her.

The three-unit tenement on Wentworth Street in 2017, when it had long been unoccupied. The street was renamed Boyle Street after the only remaining family on the dead end street. Nana lived in the unit on the left; the Christies lived in the middle unit. Photo by John Christie

CHAPTER 8

Johnny's here!

Despite being a second mother to her siblings throughout her school years, Kay Banaian managed to graduate from high school. However, she gave up her dream of being a secretary to instead get a better paying job in the dye room of a woolen mill.

And although she never got to be that playful child, she did finally get out of the house. In her early twenties, she met a recently home-from-the-war Irish-American in the mill where they both worked, and on Thanksgiving Day 1946, at age 23, she married him. The newlyweds moved into a small apartment at the other end of Dover from Wentworth Street. Probably for the first time in her life she was free of the duties and obligations of being a premature mother, of having had to grow up too fast.

She had left her home and the years of being the backup mother, but she didn't leave everything behind. A need to make up for those deprived years came with her, as did a faith that the shadow that had fallen on her from her mother's tragic life would be lifted. And it was… until one day decades later it returned with a vengeance.

A year and a month after her marriage, I was born to Koharig "Kay" "Quod" and Thomas Henry Christie, a man who had his own deep source of sadness as I discovered in the course of investigating my past.

On the day of my birth, the calendar turned over and my family got a fresh start. The date was Jan. 1, 1948 and my family was delivered an antidote for the past. An antidote to that murder in a Turkish village, an antidote to the death of a father just starting to live the American dream, an antidote to two world wars and the Depression.

On that New Year's Day, just two years after the end of World War II, John Thomas Christie offered Nana and my mother and father — and my mother's siblings — a life not forged by massacres, wars and poverty.

Someone had to be the un-victim. Someone was destined to have a life free of tragedy, worry and even much responsibility.

That's how I came to be the Prince of Wentworth Street — where my parents had moved from their small apartment across town shortly after I was born.

Home for me until I was 12 was in the middle unit of that same three-unit building where my mother had grown up, on a dead-end street in a mill town of about 20,000 people in the 1950s. There were only four buildings on Wentworth Street. One was an abandoned home across from our tenement, most of its windows broken by boys like me throwing rocks. A grumpy old man from the family that gave the street its name lived in another building, a two-story house with peeling paint and stuffed birds visible through the windows. A large Irish family — the Boyles — lived in a third building, located at the bottom of the rutted street. Beyond them was Poppy's Field, once a grazing pasture and now an empty lot where the kids in the neighborhood played pickup baseball, sledded in winter and dammed up streams in the spring.

In the middle of the street, which was just a couple hundred yards from the city's Main Street, sat the fourth building, a rust-colored tenement, though not of the type you find in big cities, with each unit atop the one below. The apartments — each with a cellar, a first and second floor and an attic — lay side-by-side.

One end unit was rented; my mother, father, brother and I lived in the middle unit, which we rented from the landlord, my mother's mother, my Nana; Nana and the five adult children who hadn't yet left the nest lived in the last unit. They were my second family.

43

With their demanding physical jobs — one on the day shift, one on the second shift — my parents often had only enough time and energy to provide the basics of what I needed in the way of care and feeding. But time to read to me, to have me sit in their lap, to fuss over me, was in short supply. For that I could always go to the other side of that tenement wall where I had another family of "mothers" and "fathers," who treated my arrival at their door as an event each time I showed up, even though I had been there just the day before and would be back the day after.

They were the people I called Nana, Army Mae, Aunt Lity, Uncle Licky, Uncle George and Uncle Dean — my mother's mother and her two sisters and three brothers. Every day, sometimes more than once a day, I would leave our apartment, take two steps down to the sidewalk, turn right, walk two steps up and open the door to Nana's apartment.

"Johnny's here!" one of them would exclaim.

"Do you want a glass of milk and some Toll House cookies? They're just out of the oven."

Next door I could always find stacks of Golden Books in which toy tugboats are rescued and returned to a boy's bathtub and a poky little puppy learns not to dig holes if he wants dessert.

"Did you bring that book with you? Sit on my lap and read it to me. Do you see how good he reads? He's a real Professor Shingle-dingle."

I was the beneficiary of a phenomenon that was much praised until its demise, when it was much mourned: the extended family. I never heard that term growing up, and I doubt anyone in my family had either. Why my mother and father moved just after I was born from their apartment at the opposite end of Dover to the apartment next to my mother's family I don't know. I doubt they had in mind providing me with all the advantages of a highly touted sociological phenomenon. The reason probably had everything to do with the fact that with both of them working, they realized the importance of living where there was always going to be someone available next door when they needed a babysitter.

But I was over there even when my mother or father was home because in Nana's house I was treated like a prince — or perhaps I should say a god, because, as God named the animals, I named my aunts. I could not say "Aunt Mary." It came out Army Mae and because little Johnny had so decreed, that was what everyone called her. Lillian, the youngest daughter, was Aunt Lity not Aunt Lillian, and to this day that's what she calls herself in her notes and emails to me. As the prince, my mispronunciations were not corrected, but acclaimed as the new proper way to speak.

If I was the prince of our street of commoners, then Nana, Army Mae, Aunt Lity, Uncles Dean, George and Licky — all (except Nana) in their late teens and twenties when my parents moved next door to them — were my courtiers, always delighted to be in my presence.

Royalty dines from a golden platter while the court jester entertains. Home from school for lunch at Nana's, I would be seated on an easy chair in front of the TV and delivered a tuna fish sandwich, some cookies and a glass of milk on a tray, while I was entertained by cartoons. Happily into my lunch, which was being served by my grandmother, I was of course unaware that she grew up in an orphanage run by German Lutherans where the children had milk just once a year — on the Kaiser's birthday.

A prince's subjects shower him with coin. The Wentworth Street version was Uncle Dean "losing" his spare change between the cushions of his chair, laughing while I dug out the pennies, nickels and dimes.

Aunt Lity was off at nursing school when we moved next door, so I didn't see much of her, but Army Mae, who was just out of high school then, was the main attraction. Army Mae taught me my numbers by having me name each step as I walked up to the second floor. But when I got to the seventh step, I never said seven. Instead, I said fun-nah. No one knew why or where it came from, but they all thought it was cute and clever and made me do it over and over.

On Saturday nights, I sat next to her while she primped for her date with her fiancé, Art, whom I was so jealous of I called him "Art the Fart." He and his brother coached a youth basketball team, but I was a year too young to be allowed to play. But princes don't have to play by the rules — Army Mae persuaded Art to put me on the team. The uniform shirt went down nearly to my knees.

When I was old enough to handle a rifle, Uncle George took me on a hunt, for squirrels and blue jays not wild boar, but like royalty we finished it off with a feast, mill-town style — doughnuts and chocolate milk.

The youngest uncle — Stephen, nicknamed Licky — was the one member of the extended family who didn't treat me as precious cargo. As I grew from toddler to boy to teenager, I also grew closer to the freewheeling Licky and could intuit why he treated me differently than anyone else did — he sensed that it was up to him to put a little bad boy in me, a little swagger.

All seemed normal on Wentworth Street. Uncles and fathers back from the war. Everyone with jobs — as dry cleaner, roofer, machinist, truck driver.

A doting Nana. And in all those years of living one door over from her, I saw little that seemed exotic or unusual about Nana. I knew nothing of her story, of why there was always a darkness in her eyes even when she was smiling and laughing.

All I knew was that I had a grandmother who gave crushing hugs, whose hands smelled of chopped onions, who sang me a rhyme in German as she bounced me on her lap, who never failed to smile at me.

She called me John Quincy Adams because she was an American now and all things were possible for her all-American grandson. Everything I did or said was so exclaimed over it was as if no other little boy had ever existed, and I was the prototype. Anything she could do for me, she did.

One of her jobs when I was a boy was working for a dry cleaner as a steam-presser. In the summer — when the work had to have been oppressive — I would ride my bike the mile or so to the Bourque Cleaners because I knew when I'd get there she'd reach into her big black pocketbook and give me a nickel to get a cold 7-Up from the vending machine. She'd pinch my cheek, kiss me, and then I was on my way, riding one-handed while guzzling down the soda, oblivious to her sacrifice and pain.

However, even as a boy I did not need all the details of her life to pick up what was implied by hints, by looks, by perhaps what I could taste in the stuffed grape leaves. Feelings don't need all the facts.

Her memories could almost be seen in the deep wells of the eyes that shine out from the photo of her holding me tightly in her lap: the once-starving Armenian woman and the well-fed American boy; the woman's muscled forearms, strengthened by spooling cotton in a mill and lifting presses at the dry cleaner, holding that child in an unbreakable lock.

This little one, says the photo, is safe. The Turks may come, a war may come, deprivation may come, but I will keep my grandson safe from it all.

Tragedy doesn't need explication to be sensed, to be unconsciously grafted onto your own soul. I heard things that were said and knew that they were important even though I didn't understand them. Heard my grandmother say the words "dirty Turk." Heard the word "genocide," and knew that whatever it was it was the reason Nana had lost her father.

By the time I was in high school I knew the Armenians had been victims of the Turks, as the Jews had been victims of the Nazis. But what the Nazis did to the Jews was a history I knew much better than what the Turks had done to the Armenians because Hitlter's atrocities were covered in history classes and were fodder for popular cultures — the only culture I was exposed to growing up in Dover when I did. But what happened to the Armenians wasn't mentioned in any of my classes, and it wasn't until 2017 that a single Hollywood movie was made about the Armenian Genocide.

The facts about the Armenian Genocide that had engulfed my whole family were still mostly unknown to me. In fact, they would remain so until after that trip to the Canadian wilderness, when I realized that for the sake of my relationship with Naomi, I was going to have to try to answer that question from my Catholic Catechism: Who am I?

The procession during the "May Crowning" celebration honoring the Virgin Mary, St. Mary Academy. Probably taken by my mother when I was in the third or fourth grade.

CHAPTER 9

The boy in the cashmere coat

To be the antidote to my family's suffering, I had to look the part. Especially when people were watching.

The snow banks of the winter of 1954 had receded from the streets of Dover, the trees were budding out, and it was time for the boys and girls of St. Mary Academy to put their piety on display in honor of the Blessed Virgin.

A life-sized statue of Mary, the mother of Jesus, stood on a pedestal in the paved playground of the Catholic elementary school I attended from first to eighth grade. On the first day in May that year — and every year — we marched in procession, by grade, from our classrooms to the playground where one of the older students — always a girl — would place a crown of flowers on the statue, and Father Desmond would lead us in reciting the Hail Mary.

For my mother, the May Crowning was not a religious event — she wasn't even Catholic. It was an opportunity to show off the good boy. I am dressed for the event in a crisp white shirt and a perfectly knotted tie under a light-colored cashmere sports coat that fits me as if it has been hand-tailored. My hands are posed in prayer, my full dark hair neatly combed, my head piously bowed.

I am six years old and dressed like an advertisement from a men's magazine, dressed in a manner that far exceeds my family's income, my family's social status, my family's education. We are mill-town people, factory workers living in a tenement on a dead-end street in a rough part of town in the 1950s. But my mother had used every spare cent she had to make sure I was presented to our little part of the world as the triumph over hardship, the consolation for deprivations that went back to the beginning of the century.

"You had to have the best," Aunt Lity, my mother's baby sister, has told me. "Your mother would save whatever she could from her job in the mill to buy you outfits from the best department store in Dover. She always wanted to be a snappy dresser, but never had any money. Now that she had some, she spent it on you."

It was a part of being the antidote, the good American boy.

It was an easy role to play. In my family, that meant being average, respectful and modest. It did not mean having to get straight As, doing chores, picking up after myself or standing out in any way.

No one in my family would ever have said, "Don't hide your light under a bushel basket" because, one, no one expected you to have a "light" and two, if you did, they expected you to know enough to keep quiet about it. Bragging was a kind of mortal sin.

Striving has been the theme of most immigrant coming-of-age stories. The children and even the grandchildren of immigrants are pushed to be the best at school, get into the Ivy League, become doctors or lawyers. Strive, strive, strive. The Irish found their future in mastering politics and the civil service, becoming police chiefs, mayors and, in my teenage years, even president of the United States. The children and grandchildren of eastern European Jews worked hard to get away from the peddlers' carts and sweat shops, into the professions, business and the arts. Armenian-Americans, I found out very late in life, were the only ethnic group in the country to have more post-graduate degrees than Jews.

But I felt none of that push to succeed.

By the time I began my self-investigation, few of the adults from my youth who could have explained why I was treated this way were still alive. I had come on my own to view it as a response to the tragedies of the past, especially the most traumatic, the deaths of Nana's father, mother and little brother. Everyone before me in my family had had to fight even to survive: survive the genocide, survive a war, survive poverty and the Depression. Perhaps they wanted to spare me any sense of struggle, I theorized.

And then my wife, Naomi, came across a more definitive explanation in an article by a university scholar titled, "The impact of the Armenian Genocide on the offspring of Ottoman Armenian survivors."

One second-generation Armenian-American is quoted in the article that "he had the feeling growing up that … he was such a precious item to his parents that he could not take the ordinary risks other children did at play, and he had to make sure he stayed whole and healthy."

Survivors like my grandmother, the author said, wanted their children and their grandchildren to "grow up in safety and did not want to inflict sadness onto them."

So, joyful announcements that "Johnny's here!"; admonitions not to boast, perhaps because it might not be safe to call attention to yourself; warnings to avoid all risk-taking in school or on the ball field or playground because … well, you might get hurt (which for all the other boys was just a normal part of being a boy) — all these were what I heard from the adults who took care of me and loved me. And for awhile I went along with all of it.

(When I was 70 years old and asked my oldest pal from the neighborhood what kind of kid I had been, he replied, "Oh, you were the peacemaker when there was an argument.")

No one in my family asked me to fight for anything — not for the best grades I was capable of, not for being best on the ball field, not for being the best at anything. I was never even asked to help with the dishes, shovel snow or mow the lawn.

Everything I needed was provided for. If it wasn't a lot, it was at least as much — and often more — than my family could afford. Yet, the sense of having to be on guard against the scarcity that might be just around the next corner played itself out even with me. I could have what I needed, but there could be no waste.

"Don't lose your baseball glove. You're not getting another one," my mother warned me more than once.

"Don't rip those dungarees in the playground."

"Bring your bike in before it rains."

Besides obeying admonitions like those, I had to do very little to meet my family's expectations. All they wanted for themselves and for me, and all I wanted for myself, was to blend in.

When I was about 10, however, something happened that I worried would mark me and my family as different. My mother came home wearing a big surgical collar around her neck.

She had been driving home from her job at the General Electric plant in nearby Somersworth (the woolen mill had moved to the South, where labor was cheaper), when our '55 Buick was rear-ended on the northern end of Central Avenue My mother said she had "whiplash," but it was probably something more serious given the operation she had not long after the accident. The collar they put on her at the hospital was about four inches high, faintly greenish in tint, punctured with air holes and lined top and bottom with a corded edging for comfort. It kept her head erect like the snobbish British ladies I would later see in the movies. To look sideways, she had to turn her whole upper body not just her neck.

It was alien.

It turned my mother into a thing I dreaded: the odd one out, the one who did not fit in at a time when conformity kept you accepted, safe.

No one else's mother had one of these things around her neck, and I worried it would bring attention to what else was not quite right about the Christie family. It wasn't the Christie side that worried me. My father was Irish, with a pale complexion that allowed every vein in his face to stand out. He worked in the mill, drove a used car, had fought in World War II, went to St. Joseph's Catholic Church for Sunday Mass, enjoyed a beer after supper, liked to watch the Friday night fights on TV and didn't say a helluva lot. All of which made him just like everyone else's father in Dover, N.H.

His full name was Thomas Henry Christie. And that, of course, was fine, too. But my mother's name was Koharig. It was a strange name in a city of Irish, whose daughters were named Mary and Barbara and Peggy, and French-Canadians, whose daughters were Janet and Ann and Patricia. So strange that she simply made up a new name for herself — Kay. But even as "Kay" my mother stood out from the rest because she did not have the northern European look of the Irish and Scots-English of New England or even the darker southern European look of the French. Instead, she and her brothers and sisters had the black eyes that stare out from every photo I've ever seen of an Armenian, as well as the cured tobacco complexion and a face dominated by a nose both wide and long. My mother's brother, George (named for Nana's savior), had a nose that my son, Nick, recalls he looked upon with awe.

So I went around hoping the kids in the neighborhood, the kids at St.

Mary Academy, as well as the nuns and priests, would focus on my last name — even, perhaps, on those auspicious initials — J.C. That might distract them from the fact that perhaps I had a slightly darker complexion than most of the kids and a mother who was not Catholic and didn't go to any church at all, never mind "the right one."

When kids my age asked me, "What are you" and I replied honestly (I was never a denier of my family), "I'm Irish and Armenian" — I hoped they would just register the first part, but often they would come back with, "What's an Armenian?"

I didn't know much, but I knew where Armenia was on the map.

"It's part of Russia," I'd say.

I see now that that explanation probably didn't go over so well since these were the days of the Cold War with the Soviets, of atom bomb drills and the Cuban missile crisis.

(I was right — and I was also wrong — about Armenia being in Russia. It was true that when I was a boy the Republic of Armenia was a part of the USSR. It became an independent nation only in 1991. What I was wrong about — and didn't understand until I started on this research — is that the Hovsepians never lived in the Armenian Republic. They lived hundreds of miles away from there, in a section of Turkey that was once long ago ruled by Armenians.)

In the 1950s, in a New Hampshire mill town, 10-year-olds knew — and cared — very little about the rest of the world. Even a place as close as Boston required a mental leap. What we had on our minds was tomorrow's spelling test and staying in the good graces of Sister Mary Aloysius and her wooden ruler.

Nonetheless, it was clear to me that being part Armenian mattered. It marked me as different, especially as far as the church was concerned. Just about every boy in my class who had decent grades and good behavior — as I did — was asked to be an altar boy. This was what passed for prestige in our set. The altar boys had their own uniforms, those black and white gowns, and were around the altar all through the Mass, assisting the priest, where they could be seen and respected by every Catholic in the parish. They were *this* close to the Eucharist — the communion wafers, which Catholics believe is the body and blood of Christ, our savior.

For some unstated reason, I wasn't allowed to get that close. I hadn't the confidence to ask why not. You had to be a bold child indeed to question the priest or the nuns and if you did, instead of an answer to your impertinence, you'd get a sarcastic comeback or that wooden ruler. In any case I didn't need to ask because the reason seemed obvious: I came from a "mixed marriage," marking me as less Catholic than everyone else.

Officially, I was a 100-percent baptized Catholic, but the nuns and the parish priest — the ones who could have made me an altar boy — no doubt knew those dark-skinned people in that tenement on Wentworth Street were not full-fledged members of the "one, true apostolic church."

The grape arbor my grandmother had planted at the bottom of a small hill in our backyard was yet another thing that marked us as different. For while anyone else would have grown grapes for the fruit, Nana grew them for the leaves. Who else but these people who came from some unheard-of place in Russia, land of godless commies, ate leaves? We did, stuffed with lamb and rice and cooked slowly in tomato sauce and eaten alongside bread that was not Wonder, but was round and flat like a pancake. Decades later, it would become fashionable to eat pita bread, but when I was a boy it was so "other" that my mother made sure the sandwiches I took to school were never made of pita, but of the same tasteless, soft white bread everyone else ate.

Yet no Wonder Bread sandwich could disguise our differentness. My mother's neck brace, her foreign name, the exotic land of her family, the flat bread and the stuffed grape leaves — all of these made me even more determined to be the All-American boy, even if I couldn't quite be seen as the all-Catholic boy.

I played all the normal sports, collected baseball cards, read Boy's Life magazine, was quartermaster of my Boy Scout troop, built model planes and cars, spent my spare change on military surplus at the Army & Navy store, camped, climbed trees just for the joy of it and put decals of bathing beauties on the fenders of my Schwinn bike.

These experiences could all be acquired with a few coins or a birthday present or by signing up for Scouts or Little League.

But I couldn't buy my way out of being the good boy, the deferential boy, the one raised by the descendants of genocide, wars and money struggles who were determined I live a life free of any conflict or struggle. As a result, I was not prepared for the normal tussles of boyhood.

One day when I was somewhere between the ages of 10 and 12 I was walking home after visiting my father's family in another working-class section of Dover. A boy about my age, but a little smaller, was walking towards me on the sidewalk. Just as he got to me, without saying a word, he punched me in the face, and I nearly fell down. For a moment, I was in shock, confused as much as hurt. By the time I recovered, he had resumed walking on his way, not even bothering to run from me, not afraid I would strike back.

"Why did you do that!" I yelled to him. To his back, really.

He didn't bother to answer.

And I didn't bother to go after him.

I was unwilling to return a punch, much less throw the first punch.

Why wasn't I tougher, why didn't I give as good as I got, why didn't I assert myself on the playground? Because even though I was raised in a town and a neighborhood and a time in which boys were expected to be fighters, that kind of aggression was tempered in me.

The only time I willingly sought out a fight was on the basketball court, where I fouled out of most of my high school games because it was the one place where I felt safe enough — and confident enough — to express the aggression expected of any red-blooded male.

I knew I had to be the good boy, the prince of Wentworth Street, even though I never used those words. But why was my family so invested in it? I had no idea back then, and no thoughts about what else I should be.

A time would come when I would be ripe for shedding that identity. But before that there were more lessons to be learned about how to be the good boy, and many opportunities to learn them.

It was a period when the institutions that taught and enforced moral behavior — family, church, Boy Scouts and others — were strong and trusted. They are in various stages of disrepair and disrepute now, but when I was the prince of Wentworth Street, they ruled my world.

St. Mary Academy, Dover, N.H., founded in 1912 and still operating as an elementary school.

CHAPTER 10

Scout's honor

At the end of each school week, the boys and girls at St. Mary Academy were marched a half mile up Central Avenue to St. Joseph Catholic Church, which I attended every Sunday. Single file, boys on the outside of the sidewalk, girls on the inside. Heads bowed. No talking. First offense: A glare from Sister like an eagle eyeing carrion. Second offense: Plan to get a wooden-rule knuckle whack when you were back in the classroom.

It was time to confess our sins.

Before we left for confession, the nuns prepped us by reviewing, one by one, each of the Ten Commandments.

"Boys and girls, put your heads down and consider if you have violated the First Commandment since your last confession. Have you honored our Lord? Have you been a good Catholic?"

Fifty boys and girls — classes were huge in those baby boomer years — sitting in rows of wooden desks, rested their heads on their arms that they have crossed on the top of the desk. We think about our sins — were we good Catholics? Did we have any false gods before us since last Friday? Perhaps, if we are not the perfect junior saint, our minds wandered to baseball or Mary Lee, the cutest girl in the class.

In the classroom, a silent minute goes by and Sister moves on to the next commandment: Have we taken the Lord's name in vain? Here, there were likely some takers, for there were few homes, including mine, where a parent's default "swear" was not, "Jesus, Mary and Joseph!" And if your mother or father said it, well, those rougher kids among us picked it up to sling around the playground out of Sister's earshot.

(In the seventh grade, I heard a tall girl with tight curls — I can still picture her — say, "Shit." I had never heard anyone but an adult say that before, and I was 12 years old. I was shocked.)

Commandment No. 3: Failure to go to church every Sunday and on the Holy Days might have found a few sinners among the boys and girls who came from the wrong side of the tracks and whose parents didn't get them up every Sunday, force them into their best clothes to sit — and kneel and stand — the excruciating 60 minutes of the Mass.

Until the eighth commandment, the "shalt nots" made some sense to us, whether we were six years old in the first grade or 13 in the eighth grade. But No. 8 threw me and everyone else, I assume: Thou shalt not commit adultery.

Here was a nun — often a young woman who had entered the convent right out of high school — asking us if we had committed an act that was a mystery to us and probably barely understood by her.

Yet, we put those heads back on the desks and waited quietly until Sister went on to No. 9 — have we coveted our neighbor's wife? I knew my mother complained about the skimpy outfits of the woman who lived kitty-corner from us on Henry Law Avenue.

"She's just showing off for the men," my mother said, when the woman walked around her yard in shorts and a top that exposed a few inches of her belly.

My father said nothing.

Maybe he was coveting? Or was it my mother doing the coveting, whatever that was? I was pretty sure it wasn't something I was doing, so I didn't confess to that or adultery, although I bet a few kids did and that that made for a good laugh for the priest.

In any case, we kept all our confessions — whatever they were — to ourselves until we entered the confessional, that oaken box the size of a closet where a priest sat on one side and we kneeled on the other, awaiting the moment of truth when Father would slide open the yellow-tinted window and say, "Yes, my son." And then you began, planning to confess just enough to appear normal for your age and not enough to induce his wrath. One girl made the mistake of asking Father if it was a sin to French kiss. You could hear him yelling, "French kiss! Of course, it is a sin!"

St. Mary Academy, which I entered at age five, the youngest in my class, and graduated from at age 13, was a three-story red brick monolith that squatted on Dover's central artery. The playground was an L-shaped expanse of rough asphalt surrounded by a chain-link fence. When the morning whistle blew, we obediently broke away from our playground cliques and lined up by grade and gender and entered the school up the wide staircase, hung our coats on hooks in the hallways and took our assigned seats. All sternly overseen by those black obelisks that were our teachers.

Together, St. Mary's and home (and the Boy Scouts) formed me into the good boy — the humble boy, the deferential boy, the respectful boy. These norms were universal in the 1950s and early 60s, just overemphasized in my upbringing. At home, there was rarely a swear word, no complaining was allowed, arguing with my little brother got me a sharp "Stop it!" Meanwhile, I saw my father head to work wearing the same cheap jacket all winter long, my mother get her entertainment from the free crafts classes held by the local university, so I counted myself lucky that I was not the kid in school with patched pants and a lunch of greasy leftovers.

While in the course of this self-investigation, I came across a novel featuring another "good boy" and found a passage that perfectly expressed the dynamic at work in producing such a creature.

"Swede" — the nickname for Seymour Levov — is the tortured good boy of Philip Roth's "American Pastoral." It covers a slightly different era — perhaps 10-15 years before my coming of age. But little changed in that interim, especially in New Hampshire, where "advances" in mores lagged greater New York, the milieu of Roth's (aka Nathan Zuckerman's) youth.

What made Swede and his schoolmates the people they were? Roth writes that their obedience was ensured by "the enacted ideology of parental self-sacrifice that bled us of wanton rebelliousness and sent underground almost every indecent urge."

Yes, the knowledge of my parents' self-sacrifice had a powerful effect on my good-boyness. Two outside agencies — my parochial schools (elementary and high school) and my Catholic Boy Scout troop — reinforced it. Any impulse to "sin" — to utter a swear word, to indulge an "impure thought," to disobey any of the authority figures that loomed over me — was countered on all sides.

The proscriptions of the time and place were even codified in the two books that were the staples of my earliest years, the assigned reading from the school and the Scouts: the Baltimore Catechism and the Boy Scout Handbook.

There were no other books in my home except the "World Book," a cheap encyclopedia my parents got for us to use for school papers. I never saw my father, with his education that stopped at age 16, read anything but the newspaper. My mother read "Life" and "Look" and the "Saturday Evening Post," but never a book.

One day when I was in my 40s and was visiting my mother, I went up to the second-floor bedroom I had shared with Gary, a finished attic space with slanted walls covered in dark paneling. As I was looking around — I think I was searching for the shoeboxes of baseball cards I had collected when I was a kid because I wanted to share them with my son — I came across two items from my past: Not the baseball cards I was looking for, but a catechism and the Boy Scout Handbook.

Since then, I have flipped through those worn pages many times, sniffing the odors of our home — the humid attic, the decades of Dad's Lucky Strikes and Mom's Pall Malls — and finding words and images that explained myself to me.

In both books, boys are depicted as wholesome, cheerful, sincere, humble. The catechism chapter on penance opens with a large black-and-white drawing of a boy in jacket and tie, his face beaming, his hands clasped at his chest. Red lines radiate from his body as they do in the drawings of Christ and the saints. The quote above his head states, "I always feel grand after confession."

It had been more than 50 years since I had first seen this drawing, but I remember dwelling on it, comparing my looks with the saintly dark-haired boy, thinking I looked a little like him and feeling less "other."

The catechism was not only a primer in Catholic doctrine, but also a guide to behavior, to putting the theology into practice.

The Fourth Commandment is, "Honor thy father and thy mother." The catechism (there were editions for each grade level; the higher the grade, the more detailed the catechism) extrapolated much more from those simple words given to Moses: "Children respect their parents when they pay them due reverence, speak and act with proper deference, accept their corrections readily, seek their advice regarding important decisions, and bear with charity their parents' faults."

According to the Catholic Church, the Fourth Commandment refers not just to the authority at home, but to all authority: "All are obliged to respect and to obey legitimate civil and ecclesiastical authorities when they discharge lawfully their official duties."

The lessons from that commandment went even further, into the world of politics: "A citizen must love his country (and) show a sincere interest in his country's welfare by voting honestly and without selfish motives, by paying just taxes and by defending his country's rights when necessary."

Here, perhaps, was the beginning of a social conscience, one that led me to major in political science and philosophy and a career as a journalist specializing in government and investigative reporting. One of my first newspaper stories exposed a city councilor who had taken a bribe from investors in return for voting for a zoning change to develop a large tract of farmland.

The greatest commandment, of course, is the simplest: to love God and love your neighbor as you love yourself. The catechism interpretation told us that to obey that commandment we must perform works of mercy. When I was in my 50s, I was at a major league baseball game in Kansas City and had gone to get a beer when I came across a man under the stands beating up another man. He had him down on the concrete floor, slugging him over and over again in the head. People were standing around watching. I pushed my way into the crowd and dragged the victim away.

I am not a brave person, but I think now that what I heard year after year at St. Mary Academy and at home made me an empathic person. Without consciously acknowledging it to myself, I had internalized my family's history as innocent victims. When I saw the man being beaten, I instinctively identified with him and was rescuing myself and my Nana as much as him.

The catechism defined acts of mercy also as "to bear wrongs patiently" because Christ forgave those who nailed him to the Crucifix ("Forgive them Father, for they know not what they do.")

In practice, that came to mean that I was never allowed to blame anyone but myself for my failings. The teacher was always right; the boss was always right; the coach was always right.

Me: "Sister Basil yelled at me for talking in class, but I was just telling Donald Phipps to stop poking me with his ruler."

My mother: "You should have waited until after class to talk to Donald. It's not Sister's fault. She has a lot of you kids to keep in line."

Me: "We were singing Christmas carols today and Sister Aloysius told me and another boy to stop singing because we were ruining the song."

My mother: "Well, I guess you don't have a very good singing voice. Nobody in our family can carry a tune."

Around the age of 11, after six years of the Baltimore Catechism, I became enthralled with a new "bible." The "Boy Scout Handbook," 1959 edition, came with a heavy, indestructible cover, illustrated by Norman Rockwell. The red-headed Scout on the cover is in full uniform, down to the khaki spats. He's striding forward, one hand holding his Handbook, and facing the reader with an innocently open face that expresses all 12 points of "The Scout Law."

This idealized boy is most certainly trustworthy, loyal, helpful, friendly, courteous, kind, obedient, cheerful, thrifty, brave, clean and reverent. I wanted to be like him, and I figured I had a good head start on most of those qualities and the ones I wasn't sure of — brave? — I could try for an opportunity to acquire.

I liked being a Scout. Hiking, camping, the jamborees where we competed to start a fire without matches, wearing that pressed and creased uniform to school on the days we had patrol meetings — all were just plain boy fun. It was another place to belong and one where there was a new way to keep score — not grades like in schools or runs and hits like playing ball, but the chance to earn and get merit badges. A chance to be a "man in uniform" like my dad had been and like the heroes we saw in WWII movies.

But more was happening than progressing from Tenderfoot to Second Class to First Class. Between the handbook's sections on knot-tying, the Morse Code and how to pack a knapsack, there were instructions on living. Instructions that added up to one simple idea: being honorable. Probably a good many Scouts skipped over all the philosophy in the handbook and went straight to how to use an ax. In my case, perhaps it was the expectation at home that I be the good boy, perhaps it was an extension to the weekly review of Ten Commandments, but by the time I was around 12, I was primed for what I see now was a full-fledged code for living.

Here is the first paragraph in The Scout Law (I still have my Handbook, copyright 1959):

"A Scout's honor is to be trusted. If he were to violate his honor by telling a lie or cheating or by not doing exactly a given task when trusted on his honor, he may be directed to hand over his Scout badge."

The scout ethos implied that there is an innate sense in every boy to want to live up to the 12 virtues.

Don't be trustworthy only when you can get credit or brave only when someone is watching. A true Scout — and, it is implied, a true citizen — does what is right for its own sake. If everyone is trustworthy, helpful, courteous and kind, everyone benefits.

Studying philosophy at the University of New Hampshire, the one philosopher I understood instinctively was Rousseau. His social contract (citizens give up some rights in return for shared freedom) is not so far away from this requirement to obtain the Boy Scout's Citizenship merit badge (which I had earned):

"List and explain at least five privileges and forms of protection you enjoy as a citizen in your community, and describe your obligations to the community."

I ate up everything the Boy Scouts could offer me, but as puberty started kicking in another big idea pushed its way into my psyche, an idea as strong and ancient as the inner voice that says, "Do the right thing." The idea was to be a boy, not with halo overhead, but with torn jeans, dirty hands, bloody nose and secrets. Not just boy, but male, having a life independent from schools, church and home.

I was starting to think about shedding the tight-fitting skin I was fitted with back in Wentworth Street. All that I learned at home and from the Baltimore Catechism and the Boy Scout Handbook would stay with me and help define me as an adult. But between childhood and adulthood there was a gap to be filled.

My younger brother, Gary, and me with our Uncle Licky.

CHAPTER 11

A man named Licky

"There are always uncles …"
— Dylan Thomas, "A Child's Christmas in Wales"

I am 10 or 11 years old, riding shotgun in a delivery van, and the man at the wheel is singing a Sinatra tune while tailgating the car in front of us. That alone is enough to tell you that it is not my father driving, which he did cautiously and in silence.

The man at the wheel is my uncle, an uncle out of the book of uncles, an uncle like the cigar-smoking uncles in a Welsh parlor, the uncle that every "good boy" should have so he can see how to be one of the guys.

"Fairy tales can come true, it can happen to you, if you're young at heart," he croons as we cross Dover's upper square on a summer evening. He is my young-at-heart uncle, the uncle whose role models are not priests or saints, but men like Frank Sinatra and President Harry S Truman.

Where my father was the sober example of manly self-sacrifice, decency and reliability, Uncle Licky — from his exotic nickname to his lifelong bachelorhood — showed me another way to be a man.

My uncle was the closest thing we had to a Rat Pack character in Dover, circa 1960. Stephen "Licky" Banaian was not slender under a jaunty fedora like Sinatra, but short, stocky and swarthy, so dark that his nickname from childhood was "Licorice Stick"— later shortened to "Licky" and, to his very best friends, he was just plain "Lick."

They didn't look the part, but he and his bachelor pals constituted a local version of Sinatra's gambling, boozing and womanizing pals. Licky and friends drank hard stuff at the Elks club, gambled at the track, played golf, rented a beach house in the summer where the parties were local legend, wore snazzy shirts and adopted an air of insouciance, although I'm sure with their high school educations — or less — they had never heard the word.

To be the worldly men they wanted to be — even in a northern New England mill town where the most worldly thing you ever saw was a pocket handkerchief — they talked like they had seen it all, even if they hadn't. They were men of no doubts, their opinions firm, expressed with finality.

"Harry S Truman — you know what the 'S' stands for?" Licky asked me more than once, never waiting for my reply. "Nothing, Johnny! Nothing!"

It seemed to please Uncle Licky that Truman was the kind of man who couldn't be bothered with a middle name.

"Best president, no contest. Dropped the atom bomb on the Japs. He had guts. You know what he said, right? 'The buck stops here' and 'If you can't stand the heat, get out of the kitchen.'"

He admired Truman to the point of having a tailor make him an overcoat modeled after the one Truman was often seen wearing.

"I'm a leg man," he told me when I was a little older. "Some guys go for the other stuff," he said, figuring as a young man I didn't need to be told what the "other stuff" was. He was disappointed in me when I brought a girlfriend around to meet the family. "Her legs are too skinny," he told me later, with the unstated suggestion I do better the next time.

One day we were driving to a family picnic in his Chevy, which prompted him to give me his singular advice about car maintenance.

"You know how they tell you to change the oil in a car after so many thousand miles? It's a scam. I never change the oil in my car. If it's low, I put in a quart. There's no point in spending all that moola to change it. It's oil, for Christ's sake."

He liked ketchup on everything, from cottage cheese to ice cream and would be glad to prove it to you.

If he didn't like something, he always said the same thing: "That's my idea of nothing at all."

He ate only one meal per day, dinner. The rest of the day he subsisted on coffee and cigarettes.

Except for a short stint in the Army, he lived his whole life with his mother, my Nana. He took care of her — she never learned to drive a car, so Licky (or my mother or Army Mae) would drive her to her errands. And she took care of their apartment and cooked for him.

Each night, she would make him one of her great meals — stuffed grape leaves, or pork chops, or lamb and green beans. At the end of the meal, it was his habit to assess the quality on a dollar basis.

As he rose from the kitchen table, Nana would await his verdict.

"A buck eighty-nine, Ma."

"Two-fifty, Ma."

"A buck and a half, Ma."

And her reply was always the same. She'd exclaim his Armenian name — "Stefan!" — and slap him across the head.

Despite his admiration for the Rat Pack, he didn't get to their home ground, Las Vegas, until he was in his fifties. When he came back, he pulled me aside and, with a rare glint in his usually world-weary eyes, announced, "Johnny, you can get anything you want any time of the day or night," he said, adding with even more emphasis, "Anything."

He walked like a bow-legged John Wayne, a slow, rolling gait; his arms hung away from his torso, curved and muscle-bound, ready to pick up a bundle of newspapers in each hand and swing them into the delivery truck he drove each night. Many evenings, right after dinner, I would go with him on one of his runs, listening to him singing "Young at Heart" as he drove one of those trucks loaded with the late edition Boston newspapers.

Uncle Licky's place of work was Dover News, a distribution center for Boston and New York newspapers, magazines, comic books and paperback books. After being delivered to the Dover News warehouse on Third Street, they'd be broken down into bundles headed for newsstands and convenience stores throughout New Hampshire and parts of Maine. All day long and into the evening the bundles of Record American and New York Times newspapers and Life and Post magazines and Sgt. Rock and Batman comics and paperbacks with lurid covers were loaded into vehicles, destined for a newsstand in Sanford, Maine, a neighborhood market in Dover, a coffee shop in Durham frequented by professors from the University of New Hampshire, etc.

Uncle Licky was the shop foreman. But he also dug in and did the hands-on work. He'd schedule the drivers and bundlers, coordinate the orders he got from the office "girls" with the work on the warehouse floor, hire and fire, and when the day's work was supposed to be done, he'd run the last route of the day himself, which is where I came in.

Usually, he'd double-park in front of the store, grab a stack of newspapers, hurry into the store and drop the papers on the counter. That took a minute or two and then on to the next stop. Sometimes, Licky wanted to do the evening route a little faster and get to wherever he was going that night — the Elks or the track — so he would recruit me to help him. When we got to the stop, he'd hand me a stack of newspapers, and I was to run in as fast as possible, drop the papers and get back in the van. I took it as a challenge and a game — and a way to show off to my uncle.

While he was driving — too fast — he'd reach over with his right hand to the stack of papers on the center console, count out the papers for the next stop and hand them to me. Just as he pulled up — but before he had come to a complete stop — I'd open the door and get ready to leap out, zig-zag between parked cars, likely cut off a customer entering the store, slap the stack on the counter and speed back to the car, leaping into the front seat and closing the door just as Licky sped off.

I was never allowed to play organized football — my father was worried I'd get hurt — but I longed to be a swivel-hipped halfback like Paul Hornung, the Notre Dame and Green Bay Packers star who twisted and turned his way though the defensive line, head-faked linebackers and outran the safeties. My evening runs with Uncle Licky were as close as I got to that dream.

A stack of Record Americans were my football, black low-cut Converse sneakers my spikes, Fords and Chevies the defensive line and a mother pushing a baby carriage the final defender in my way as I scooted downfield into City Hall Market for an easy first down, dropping the papers precisely in their assigned spot.

All that was missing was the cheering. Instead what I got was a critique.

"Seven seconds, Johnny. Not bad," Uncle Licky pronounced when I got back in the van. "You can do better on the next stop."

I doubt he really timed me, but the fact that he was never all that impressed with me was a different experience from what I had at home. Licky didn't think he needed to go easy on me, didn't see me as an antidote to the

Armenian Genocide that had killed the grandfather he never met.

Licky seemed to have put all that in a compartment and then gone on to be a full-fledged American, even if he had to accept — and embrace — the fact that his foreign complexion was so defining it had literally changed his name.

When I was in college, Licky gave me a paying job at Dover News. I came to the warehouse right after dinner every Saturday night.

Trucks and vans were parked inside. Long folding tables with scarred wooden tops lined the concrete floor, lit by a series of bare bulbs hanging from the ceiling rafters. It smelled of millions of tons of sulfurous newsprint that had passed into and out of the warehouse over the years. I was dabbling in journalism in college, but had no way of knowing then that newsprint — the cheap paper on which every newspaper that ever was is printed — would become the canvas on which my whole life would be painted.

The work started on the tables, where we lined up the different sections of the Boston Sunday newspaper that had arrived in the past couple of days. The sections that are not filled with breaking news and sports are printed ahead, sections like the weekly magazine, the comics, lifestyle, business, etc. Early Saturday evening, the live sections arrived. But, as I learned then, no one wants their Sunday papers in six different pieces. The pieces have to be put together into one package, a job called stuffing or inserting.

Late on Saturday, the final sections — the news and sports — showed up and we inserters put the various pieces together in one package, with the front section — page one — on the outside.

We lined up the Boston Globe sections in front of us — a stack of feature sections, a stack of advertising flyers, a stack of business sections, etc. and the final stacks — news and sports. We'd shuffle quickly along the line, working as fast as possible, grabbing each section and then opening up the final section and shoving the other sections in it. The completed Globes sat at the end of the table and when that stack reached a certain number, we gathered it up by both arms, stood the stack on its end to even out the pile and then brought it over to the baling machine. Here, we looped heavy wire around the stack and then fed the two ends into a device with a lever. We pulled on the lever and the ends were twisted into a tight braid at the top, and we loaded the bundle onto a truck or van.

Licky supervised all of us, and when we got behind he'd stand at a table and show us how it was done. He could do a row in three or four seconds, his right hand grabbing sections and his left hand reaching at the same time for the final section. Swish, swish, swish and slap — a completed package.

When the Boston papers were ready, they were loaded into a large delivery truck driven by one of the fulltime employees. I helped load the truck and went along to do just what I did when I was 10 years old — get the news to the storefronts as fast as possible. The run was done between midnight to 3 a.m., when the stores were closed, so I dropped the bundle at the door.

When that run was over, we'd get back to the warehouse and by then all the other inserters had gone home. The last sections of the New York Times had arrived while I was doing the Boston-paper run, and it was left just to me to stuff the copies of the Times, load them into a van and deliver them. I had started around 7 p.m. and by now it was 7 or 8 a.m. and my long shift would end when I finished the Times run.

I was grateful for the job and the thirty bucks or so I made each week, but I was even more gratified by the compliment that Uncle Licky — prototype in my mind of a man-about-town — had enough confidence in me to have me work alongside him and the other regulars and trust me to do that final run on my own.

Week after week, including many when I had to maneuver that van through New Hampshire snowdrifts, nothing ever went wrong. The right number of Times went to the correct stores at the correct time, the van was returned to the shop undamaged, the shop then locked and secured for re-opening on Monday.

Licky was the one adult in my family who expected something from me. He expected me to run fast, to have a girlfriend with great legs, to be intimate with the "other stuff" a woman is made of, to be able to imagine what went on in Las Vegas, to keep up with working men, to drive a delivery van in any weather. He even expected me to sing to remind myself to stay young at heart.

Like he was.

The Christie's new home at 167 Henry Law Ave., Dover, N.H.

CHAPTER 12

Up from the tenement

My mother's car accident was worth a house. That's what the insurance settlement bought. It also bought her years of pain, so bad that she had an operation that removed part of a bone from her right leg to use to repair the damage to her spine. I'll forever be able to visualize the long scar on her leg and the stitches like the laces on a football. I was impressed that my very own mother was the subject of such advanced and gruesome surgery.

"My mother had part of her leg removed and put into her back," I told the kids in the neighborhood. I wanted to impress them, and in the days of The Twilight Zone and Superman comics, I thought having a mother with a leg bone in her back was different in a good way, as opposed to having a family that ate leaves and came from a mysterious land in Russia.

We moved on a sunny day in June, 1959. I was 11 years old, just finishing the seventh grade. Gary was three years behind me. The big news of the moment was Castro taking over Cuba, but that sort of news did not penetrate the mind of a boy in dungarees and a striped t-shirt who was out of school for the summer and moving into a real house, not a tenement. It wasn't up to the standards for a middle class home set by what we saw on our favorite TV shows, but we weren't middle class and never would be.

The homes and the parents in "The Donna Reed Show," "Leave to Beaver" and "Father Knows Best" were as distant and fantastic to me as anything from the Twilight Zone. Those families lived in large, white homes on tree-lined streets, not dark tenements with rudimentary bathrooms. But it was not the buildings that seemed most foreign to me. Even more unimaginable were the parents. The fathers all wore suits to work and went to an office. At that point, the only office I had ever seen was on TV. The mothers were coiffed, pale and wore dresses and heels at home, not the starched green uniform my mother wore to the GE plant. Many social critics have commented on how these shows depicted an idealized America, creating a damaging rift between what was real — where people like us lived — and what was just Hollywood fantasy. But I didn't look at those shows and think, "Well, that's not how it really is." Nor was I made to feel inferior by what I saw. Instead, I was inspired. I thought: Somewhere, sometime, that will happen for me.

There was a house in a better Dover neighborhood that did look like one of the TV homes: white clapboards, shiny black shutters, a wide lawn, a garage with a basketball backboard attached and a paved driveway to practice layups, jump shots and my running hook shot. I think a lawyer lived there — no one we knew. If we had a house like that, I told myself, I could practice my game until I could make a layup with either hand and get nothing but net over and over again from the top of the key. If we had a house like that, we might get into the mysterious group I was starting to hear about: the middle class. I didn't resent it; I wanted it.

But I also knew that for the moment it was as much a fantasy as my others: to be asked to be an altar boy, to punch the nose of the nun's favorite boy in the class, to be the top scorer in my next league basketball game.

If you walked to the end of Wentworth Street, crossed Poppy's Field, forded a stream and climbed over a barbed wire fence, you would be at our new house — 167 Henry Law Ave., my home from age 11 to when I went away to college, and mother's home for the rest of her life. It's about a 10-minute journey from where we'd lived before. Ten minutes to go from tired-looking houses crowding each other on city streets to houses with yards and driveways, houses in styles nice enough that they had names, like ranch and split-level and Cape Cod.

Our new house was a gray-shingled Cape. Five rooms: kitchen, living room, two bedrooms and a cramped bathroom, but with a shower over the tub, which seemed so very modern to me. There was a paved driveway, lawn on three sides and a neighbor in an identical Cape Cod about 20 feet from the east side of the house. To the back and side of the yard was an overgrown field with neglected apple trees; across the street were more fields and a dirt road that led down to acres of woods and sand pits and the Cocheco River.

The house cost $10,000. The insurance settlement for my mother's accident provided the down payment of $2,500, which was equal to at least half of my father's annual salary as a machinist. My mother made even less at GE, so it's hard to imagine they would ever have been able to save enough for the down payment from their jobs.

When my mother died, I found the mortgage note in her papers. It was just a half-sheet of paper, unlike today's reams of documents to get a bank loan. The monthly mortgage payment was $47.85.

Our little Cape, a modest thing, would have been a comedown for the Cleavers or the Reeds. But for a man who carried a lunch pail to his job and for a woman who worked on an assembly line soldering parts on electric meters, the house was several steps up in the world. It was almost new — we were only the second family to occupy it — and it had actual hardwood floors and a living room with wall-to-wall carpeting.

We had been delivered out of a cave and into the sunlight by my mother's accident, her pain. Koharig Banaian Christie did not want to be rear-ended on Central Avenue, and it would not have happened if she hadn't been coming home from a job where she breathed lead solder every day and sometimes burned her fingers. It was like the lesson we got from the nuns and the priests: Christ suffered and died on the cross so we would be forgiven our sins and enter the kingdom of heaven. The little kingdom we entered at 167 Henry Law Ave. wasn't even quite the bottom of the middle class — more the top of the working class. But I didn't know that at the time. All I knew was that from our new house we looked across the street to a field and a river beyond, rather than an abandoned house. Our new home was our resurrection, delivered by my mother, whose suffering would, in just a few years, become a much heavier cross to bear.

Dover's lower square and the Pacific Mills, where dad worked.

CHAPTER 13

Mack's wild ride

When we moved to 167 Henry Law Ave., I was of an age to crave independence, and I was now in a place where those who had looked after me and monitored my every move — Nana, the aunts and uncles — could not simply look out their windows and see what I was doing. A door had closed, and another had opened, giving me an opportunity to move on from being the good boy.

Not only was I leaving a neighborhood, and, I hoped, an identity, but I was also moving from childhood to teenage-hood, a land I knew as much about as I did the mythical middle class. My idea of what a teenage boy was supposed to be like came from TV, programs such as the "Spin and Marty" show, where the two boys got into — and then out of — trouble.

I understood that I wasn't going to be able to make this transition on my own, by just suddenly being a teenager-in-training. I could daydream all I wanted about the boy I thought I should become, but I felt that's all it would ever be — a daydream — if I didn't put down my copy of Boy's Life magazine and start roaming my new neighborhood.

Our spot of almost-middle-class was just one hill up Henry Law Avenue from a neighborhood much like Wentworth Street, where there were parents who worked in mills or the shipyard in Portsmouth. They lived in apartments or small houses, some no more than enlarged cottages, all squeezed together on streets that led down a series of slopes to the center of town and a big brick mill and the downtown shops.

That's the neighborhood I found myself wandering to that summer of '59, a few months before my 12th birthday. I don't know what drew me there at first, but boys of that era were free to roam, by foot or bike, and run across other boys. This was a dozen or so years after the soldiers, sailors and Marines returned home from Europe and the Pacific, got married and started having kids. So anywhere you went, from Dover, N.H. to the San Fernando Valley, there were lots of other 11- and 12-year-old boys off for the summer, looking for a baseball game, riding bikes, trading a Ted Williams for a Willie Mays Topps bubblegum card or getting together on a rainy afternoon for a game of Parcheesi.

All I had to do to find them was walk down Henry Law a quarter mile, take a right at Wallingford Street and there at the curve was a group of boys. They were dribbling and passing a basketball in the street, but there was no basket, no backboard.

"You guys going down to the playground for a game?" I asked, because I loved basketball and knew I could hold my own in any pickup game and if I did, well, then, maybe I could be part of whatever this was.

The tallest one grabbed the ball, set it on a cocked hip and held it there with his arm. He was wearing what we all wore back then — dungarees, t-shirt, white sneakers. He was lean and tall and looked like he could play the game.

Everyone was waiting for his reply.

"We're going to make our own court, right here," he said, pointing at the wider curve in the street. "Come back tonight and help us."

"Hey, Mack," one of the other boys said. "We gonna go do the thing with the hood now?"

The lean boy with the basketball said, "Yeh, let's do it."

With a fluid underhand toss, he whipped the ball to one of the boys, who put his hands out just in time to avoid a shot to the chest. In the next six to eight years, I played a lot of basketball with Mack, and I learned to be ready for his passes: He'd sling the ball down court like a football, leading you by a few yards as you ran towards the basket, the ball thrown on a line like a frozen rope. The timing was perfect so that when you caught and dribbled two or three times, you were under the basket, ahead of the defender, positioned for an easy layup. Once, I wasn't prepared and the ball bounced off my hands. I still remember that glare from Mack.

The boys followed him down a driveway next to the small house where I later found out he lived with his three brothers, sister and mother. I followed, too. No one said not to, and I picked up what was in the air — this was some sort of club, or gang, even, and this lanky one was the leader.

At the end of the driveway, a detached hood from a car lay upside down. It had to have come from an older car — the hood came to a point, with tall sides, like a late 40s design. Mack went into the basement and came out with a long chain. He wrapped one end around a strut inside the hood, securing it with a double hitch, and then ran the chain further down the driveway where a green Plymouth was parked. He got down on his back and shimmied under the Plymouth and attached the other end of the chain to the undercarriage.

"Ok. Spence, you go first," Mack said.

I was getting the idea, not just of what was to come next, but also of who these kids were.

Spence lived across the street from me at the upper end of Henry Law, and I recognized him, but I didn't know him yet.

Mack tied a rope at the point of the hood, like the reins on a horse, and got behind the wheel of the Plymouth. He looked about two years older than me — not old enough to drive. A half dozen more kids, younger ones who were hanging around, jumped into the car with him.

Mack drove the car and the attached hood out to the field right behind his house and stopped at a place where the hood sat in thick grass. Spence stepped into it, grabbed the rope reins, widened his stance, leaned back and nodded his head.

Mack took off slowly, giving Spence a chance to get his balance, then drove away, dragging the upturned hood behind like a sled. Spence got cocky and let go with one hand, raising his arm to the sky like a rodeo rider on a bronco.

Mack came to the top of a hill, turned right and Spence almost negotiated the turn, but at the apex flew off into the deep grass and came up yelling, "Helluva ride boys. Who's next?"

So it went all afternoon, everyone getting their chance, unaware and indifferent to the fact that a perfectly good, registered car driven by an under-age boy was bouncing over a rutted field, that you could slip and slice

your face on the edge of the hood, or the car could stop quick and the hood
— and you — slide under the trunk.

For the kids too small to stand up on the hood, Mack would sit them
down two at a time, hand them the reins and give them a ride up and down
the hill.

They didn't have a lake, they didn't have a boat, they didn't have water skis,
but on that day, Mack had figured out a way everyone could go waterskiing
just the same.

I waited for my turn, though not sure in my diffident way if being the
newest guy I would even be offered a turn, or if I would take it if offered.
Until then, I had been avoiding danger and risk as assiduously as I'd avoided
mortal sin, venial sin and the impure thoughts the nuns and priests warned
us about, whatever they were. When I went to confession all I ever had to
confess was, "I fought with my brother." But now risk was about to present
itself, and I was going to have to make a choice.

I didn't want to come home from my new neighborhood bruised or bleeding or even with torn dungarees and have to explain myself and hear my
mother yell, "Jesus, Mary and Joseph!" and bite her fist in anger — her stan-
dard response to just about any minor infraction.

But now was the moment for the good boy to become one of the guys. I
had hoped to do that by sinking a few of my turn-around hook shots, not by
being pulled around a bumpy field by a kid in a car he shouldn't be driving
while I rode unprotected on a big hunk of metal.

No one had been hurt yet, why should I be?

"Hey, kid, new kid, your turn," Mack said.

Well, at least I was in. All I had to do was step onto this old hood, hold
on tight and, what? I was tempted to make the sign of the cross, which we
all did before we went to bat or did anything we figured could benefit from
acknowledging Jesus. But no one else had, even though they were likely all
Catholic, so I didn't either.

"Signal when you're ready," Mack said.

Then he gave me the new-kid treatment. He took off quicker than he had
for everyone else, and I was knocked on my ass, but managed to stay inside
the hood. Mack kept the pedal down until he had to ease up to make the
turn at the top of the hill, at which point I crawled up on my knees and got
hold of the reins. I was able to stand up again and make the rest of the trip
on my feet.

No one asked if I was hurt. No one said, "Sorry about that." No one treated me like the first-born grandson, the precious offspring of an oppressed minority, the consolation for a genocide. No special treatment asked, none given, just like everyone else.

In one afternoon, I had been adopted by a new family, headed by a boy only two years older than me who made up adventures and escapades, who courted trouble rather than ran away from it, who was also, as I discovered in the years to come, as brilliant in school as he was at dreaming up our schemes.

"All right, I gotta go in and eat supper now," Mack announced. "Come back when it's dark. We're gonna need a lot of help for this one."

James "Mack" McEneaney.
Photo courtesy of James McEneaney.

CHAPTER 14

How to build a basketball court

Today, every playground in even the poorest of cities has an outside basketball hoop or two. But in Dover, N.H., circa 1960, that was not the case.

The closest playground was at the bottom of Henry Law Avenue, but it was just a big open field — no swing sets, no baseball diamond, no basketball court.

So, we had to create a basketball court out of what was available and free, just as we conjured up a lake and waterskis from a vacant field and the hood of an old car.

I say "we," but Mack and Mack alone was the creative force behind overcoming these deprivations. The rest of us might have said, "Geez, I wish we had a place to play basketball." Mack didn't stop with just wishing.

And that's why he told me to come back to his house after supper that day when I showed up on his street and "waterskied" the field behind his house.

Mack had a theory about other people's possessions: If they were left unattended for a length of time — the duration of time to be determined by him — then we could assume that no one wanted them anymore, and we could take them. That's how we got our first motorcycle, a story to be told later, and our basketball court. You can't very well appropriate a basketball court, but you can make your own if you have the right parts. And thanks to Mack, we managed to get the parts we needed.

"There's a telephone pole down on River Street," he explained when I got to his house that evening. "It's been sitting there on the side of the road a long time. I went down there and measured it yesterday. If we can get it up here, we can saw it in two and those can be the posts. We'll put them right there," Mack said, pointing to the wide curve in his street.

I said to myself, "That's crazy. We'll get in trouble. That pole belongs to the telephone company. I think this is stealing."

But, I wanted to belong and kept a lid on my fears and conscience, waiting to see what the other boys would say. If one or two of them said what I was thinking, then maybe Mack would drop the whole thing and I could avoid arrest and — worse even — the stern disapproval of my parents.

I waited for the other boys to say something. But they didn't react at all. It was as if Mack had said, "Let's walk down to Jimbo's store and get a Coke." I stayed quiet and had a quick argument with myself. Go along and it could be trouble — trouble with the police, with adults who could see what we were doing, with my parents, who thought I was down here doing something like playing ring-a-levio. Sneaking around like this was not what I had been taught at home, by the Baltimore Catechism or the Boy Scout Handbook.

But the others were ready to go — Mack had their confidence. I figured this was not the first time he had come up with this sort of scheme and that they had learned he knew what he was doing. And the part of me that wasn't afraid was excited. It would be adventure, a taste of danger, our own little rebellion.

What the boys also knew — and I found out later — was that Mack was hardly a juvenile delinquent. He was one of the smartest boys in Dover High School, straight A's, an altar boy, paperboy, and math wizard who one day would spy on Russian radio conversations from a submarine in the Pacific and, later, an official with the Federal Reserve. That was years in the future, of course, but the intelligence was already in play. When he wasn't employing it in school, he was putting it to work to send a message to the world of the earnest people, the reverent people, the play-it-safe people, the ones lacking imagination. The ones who said, "You can't do that."

Yes we can, said Mack, and we'll get away with it and afterwards relive the whole thing and laugh like hell.

What was I going to do — make some excuse and walk home and lose the chance to be part of this group, part of Mack's world, which was the center of my new neighborhood?

I had stepped onto the turned-over car hood. And, after the initial panic, liked it.

I didn't say anything, just waited to see what was next, waited with that breathless anticipation that comes when you are drunk on a cocktail of fear and excitement. I would feel that many times in the future, from taking off on an "appropriated" cycle to taking a date to a drive-in movie the first time I was old enough to drive a car to waiting on a wing strut to jump out of a plane.

River Street was maybe a half-mile away and, apparently, the telephone company had left a pole along the side of the road, probably a replacement pole they intended to put up at some point. It was way too heavy to carry and even if we could have carried it, it would have taken us so long that a police cruiser on its routine patrols could have spotted us. We needed some help. We needed a truck. And Mack knew where to find one.

Ray Smith lived a few doors away from Mack. He was a jack of all trades — snow plowing, moving furniture, any odd jobs you could come up with that needed his rattle-trap Ford pickup.

Smitty might have been an adult and Mack just a teenager, but even the adults sensed this teenager was a natural leader and a superior intellect, and it didn't take much for Mack to talk Smitty into helping us.

"Jeee-suss Christ, Mack. You boys are crazy, okay. Where is this thing?" was all Smitty said, and the plan was on.

We followed him down to River Street, lifted one end of the 30-foot pole up high enough to wrap a chain around it and attached the chain to the truck so that Smitty could drag the pole all the way up Henry Law Avenue. The friction from the oil-soaked pole on the street sent up sparks and flames and left a long black mark all the way from the River Street to the front of Mack's house. The marks didn't fade for weeks, which delighted us because we knew every adult who drove up the street — and the cops — would wonder how those marks got there.

Mack had found a rim in his basement — probably something he'd taken from a school gym — and we attached it to a heavy piece of plywood to be the backboard. Then we nailed the backboard to the poles and now all we had to do was get the whole thing to stand up. We dug deep holes for the poles and used street labor — Mack, Spence, Minnie, Rube, T-Bo and me — to lift the poles into the hole. We had it in place by the end of the night.

There wasn't much time left for a practice run on the new basketball "court" — darkness was settling in. But we shot around a bit, taking jumpers, hooks, lay-ups and set shots from the asphalt street. My running hook shot — which I hoped would impress everyone — kept coming up short.

It was time to take a bigger risk.

The street was banked around the curve where the backboard was set up; the longest shot was 25 feet from the rim, right where the city had placed a storm drain. I took the ball out there — it would be three-point territory in today's game, but there was no such thing back then — and went for a shot that was so far out I could easily not only fail to sink it but might miss everything — the backboard, the rim, the net. I used a technique now long out of favor, but a classic back then and one I had practiced with success many times: the two-handed set shot. Holding the ball between your palms, you bend your knees deeply, push upwards from the squat and let her fly. Bam! — It hit the back of the rim and dropped right down through the net. I didn't say a word, just retrieved the rebound and fired a bounce pass to one of the other guys.

I was cool.

I was sure of myself.

I was in.

Now we had our own basketball court, and we played ball through all the seasons, even through the winter, shoveling out what the city did not plow away. Games of H.O.R.S.E., one-on-one, two-on-two, three-on-three and around the world. We'd bet a penny on who could make a shot; a nickel if we were feeling bold. The two-handed set from the storm drain was my go-to shot.

Many years later, well after I had moved away and the Macks had, too, I would drive by their street on the way to see my mother and look over at the curve. The basketball "court" we had made from stolen parts stood there still, the backboard gray with age, the rim rusted, the last strands of the net hanging forlornly.

It was a reminder of the day I had gone from good boy to petty thief, from take-what-life-gives-you to find-a-way-to-get-what-you-want, from "be careful" to be wild.

My dad, Thomas Christie (middle), at work at Eastern Air Devices, a precision tool-making company based in part of the Pacific Mills plant.

CHAPTER 15

Wooden nickels

In mill towns, you started work early, came home early and ate supper early. The last meal of the day was called supper, not dinner; dinner was what you ate in the middle of day, unless it was at school, then it was called lunch.

At 4:15 p.m. every day, my father would emerge from a small door in the south end of the red brick behemoth called Pacific Mills and come home to the house for supper. The mill dominated the center of town as mills like it and even bigger did in Manchester, N.H., Lawrence, Mass., Providence, R.I. and other towns large and small across New England, towns powered by an immigrant work force and an abundance of hydro electricity from the great rivers that slice through the region.

The Pacific Mills' centrality to Dover's growth from rural to industrial, from a few thousand people to 20,000, is signaled, even now, by how you get around the center of town.

Whether you come in from the south or the north, when you approach the downtown, the main road splits like a river flowing around an island. The island is the mill. Once you have driven around it, the road merges into one again.

The mill was built over the Cocheco River, which begins 30 miles upstream from Dover, and for years provided the city's power from the falls squeezed between the downtown shopping district and the mill. The river, like all the rivers of industrial America, was more a running sewer than a body of water, picking up the waste from tanneries, shoe shops, dairy farms and the effluent from homes along the river that still used outhouses. When the river ran over the falls, it revealed its true color and sent up its true odor. It pretty much smelled the way it looked — brown. In my neighborhood, when you wanted to intimidate another kid, you didn't threaten to beat him up. You said if he didn't wise up, you were going to throw him into the Cocheco.

From the mid-19th century to nearly 1940, the mill spun and wove cotton for clothes, sheets, furnishing, even toys, all printed with geometric, floral and other colorful designs under the brand Cocheco. In 1900, Cocheco mills manufactured 50 million yards of printed fabric to be sent all over the world. In 1937, the cotton mill was closed when cheaper labor and electrification in the South attracted cotton and woolen mills from all over the northeast to move to the Carolinas and Georgia. The city tried to get another large manufacturer to take over the mill, but that never happened. Instead, some sections of the complex were occupied by discrete companies, while other sections remained vacant. One of those smaller companies was called Eastern Air Devices and that's where Dad worked when I was a boy.

Each day he emerged from the tiny mouth of that whale that lay across my city, breathing the gasps of an endangered species — American manufacturing.

In the warm weather, Dad wore heavy cotton work pants, a shade of green that would hide a grease stain, and a light, short-sleeved shirt, often a pale yellow, over his white t-shirt. In the winter, he wore a cheap polyester jacket with horizontal stripes of red and yellow. I don't recall a hat to cover his wavy gray hair. He carried a black, metal lunch box, big enough for two ham sandwiches and a thermos of coffee. The middle fingers in his right hand were stained yellow from the ever-present Lucky Strikes, the crushed package with the big red circle stuffed in the breast pocket of his shirt.

I wanted his job to be something more than just plain, "My dad works in the mill," something that would separate me from everyone else, to make up, perhaps, for being the "other." And, in fact, he was more than a cog in an assembly line. His job title was "set-up man," the skilled supervisor of machinists. He used precision tools to position metal cutting machines so they would produce a perfect-fitting part for an electric motor.

That's what they did at Eastern Air Devices — make motors that went into bigger machines and jet engines. The tool he used to set up the machines was called a micrometer, a chrome device shaped like a question mark and about the size of a pair of pliers. The micrometer measured by the 1/1000th of an inch, a tolerance required for the smooth working of a motor used in an aircraft engine, for example.

"What does your dad do?"

"He's a set-up man."

I don't suppose any other kid knew what that was, but it was a title, and it was better than, "He works at the shoe shop," which was one of the worst jobs because even kids knew it didn't pay much.

One day, another boy asked me if my dad had a hobby.

A dad with a hobby? Kids had hobbies, like collecting baseball cards or making plastic models, but a grown man who works all day with his hands?

He said his father collected coins.

I had to come up with something. What does Dad do when he's not working, I asked myself. Watching the fights on TV didn't seem like a hobby.

"He paints," I said.

"Pictures?"

"No, the house."

The other boy didn't say anything.

By this time, my mother was working the day shift at GE, which got out at 3:30, so she was home in time to put supper on the table just minutes after dad got home. By 5:00 or so, we had eaten and the plates were cleared. On weekdays, supper was a variation on a monotonous theme: meat, potatoes and a canned vegetable.

The meat was usually a cube steak or a hamburger. Cube steak came from the grocery store with cube-shaped dimple marks on the surface from pounding with a tenderizing mallet. It was cheap, thin and sinewy and, in our house, cooked so there wasn't a squirt of juice left in it, if there was any to begin with. Same with the hamburgers, and when we had fresh fish, it was a thin piece of sole cooked for an hour-and-a-half at 350.

The potatoes were peeled and cut into cubes so they would boil fast and then served unadorned. The vegetable was often creamed corn.

We ate at the kitchen table — there was no dining room — which was pushed against one wall in the small kitchen. Mom sat at the end nearest the stove, about a foot away from it, Dad at the opposite end, and Gary and I on the side, Gary closest to Dad. From age 11 to when I went away to college, this was the nightly, unchanging tableau.

Was there conversation? Mom and Dad talked about whatever adults talked about: their jobs, their siblings, the neighbors, the house. Nothing that registered with me. Only one thing about their conversations stayed with me and later — when I was old enough to know a little about the opposite sex — seemed revealing. My mother didn't call my father Tom or Tommy, and he didn't call her Kay or Quod. They called each other "Babe." I assumed this went back to their days of dating, after Dad came home from the war and they both worked in the woolen mill.

"Babe" was endearing, warm, maybe even a little sexy. But I don't recall ever seeing them kiss, even on the cheek. We were not a physically affectionate family. Nana and my aunts gave many a hug, but not Mom and Dad. Now, I look back at family pictures and see my mother in a fashionable black dress, heels and a necklace and Dad in a suit and tie and pocket handkerchief, smoking a Lucky Strike like a detective from a film noir, and I realize — as children often belatedly do about their parents — that they were a man and a woman who must have been sexually attracted to each other. Calling each other "Babe" was the residue of that time, a time after the war when they went dancing every Saturday night at Simpsons restaurant or the Grange in nearby Rochester. As one of my aunts said: "They were quite a couple."

Now, however, they were the breadwinners, nice, responsible decent people, the protectors of two boys, the teachers of the life lessons they wanted us to absorb. Be respectful, honest, take care of your stuff, do your homework, obey the nuns, go to church, don't fight with each other, be home for supper and don't make a lot of noise. Dad liked it quiet and he could take only so much of my brother and me bouncing rubber balls on the roof in a backyard game of catch.

"Stop that racket," he'd yell out the window.

I can recall very few words my father ever said. When I left the house, it was always, "Don't pick up any wooden nickels." I didn't know if that meant anything more than, "Don't come home too late." It felt like something from "the olden days," and that fit well, for Dad was 35 when he got married, his family life delayed by two stints in the Army. By the time my brother Gary and I were old enough to be running around the neighborhood, Dad was in his 40s, which was middle-aged in that era. He looked even older, with hair that was all gray by the time he was married, a trait I inherited. And he had all the caution of a middle-aged man, too.

He didn't like it when I went swimming at lakes and ponds with my friends. He told me more than once that when he was a boy one of his friends had broken his neck diving into a shallow spot. "Be careful," he'd say each time I went swimming. Even today, I won't dive off a dock or a rock if I haven't jumped in feet first to check the depth. But once I joined Mack's gang, I started to take risks, and engage in other behaviors my parents would not have approved of — if they'd known about them.

Dover City Hall. Dover was settled in 1623.

CHAPTER 16

Mrs. Mack drove the getaway car

*"...there, playing Indians in the evening, I was aware of myself in the exact
middle of a living story, and my body was my adventure and my name."*
— Dylan Thomas, "The Peaches"

Every night, I'd have supper with Mom and Dad and Gary, rush though
my homework, walk down Henry Law Avenue, take a right at Wallingford
Street and there — right at the curve next to the basketball court — was the
little bungalow of the McEneaney family. The Macks.

At home, everything was the same, day after day, night after night. After supper and clean up, Dad drove to a downtown store to get the Re-
cord-American, the Boston evening tabloid newspaper, and spent the night
in his easy chair with his one nightly glass of Kruger ale and a Lucky Strike.
Mom had her Pall Mall on the breezeway, probably reading Life magazine
or a Reader's Digest. Gary was watching TV not far from my father. There
was no discussion of a plan to wreak havoc in the neighborhood or shock the
upright people.

But down at the Macks, normality was their nemesis, a memorable phrase I read later in Gay Talese's history of the New York Times. At that point in my life, normality was about all I knew. What I didn't yet know about myself was how I would respond to peers who laughed at the straight line we were supposed to walk.

The early 1960s were not yet The Sixties. It was not yet a time of general rebellion and anti-this and anti-that, especially in New Hampshire, where trends showed up late and stale. But Mack didn't need a Time magazine cover story to tell him the age of rebellion had arrived. He seemed to have been born wanting to knock the hat off Mr. Respectability. And he'd get just as big a laugh if he could walk past Mr. Respectability the next day wearing the hat and then return it to him with a sly smile.

There was never an announcement that we were to be the contrarians of Dover, N.H., no manifesto declaring we were seceding from propriety. There was just Mack saying to us, as we waited in anticipation for the next adventure: "I've got a notion."

One of his notions was a reaction to something called Club 96. Club 96 was the invention of the local radio station — a weekly dance at Dover City Hall for the "good kids." The other four percent, it was implied, were the juvenile delinquents, teenagers who stole cars, started fistfights and played hooky from school. Picture a 17-year-old boy with a pomaded ducktail haircut, black leather boots, a sneer and a dangling cigarette.

That was not Mack and that was not most of the rest of the gang. Mack didn't want to be a punk or a hood. Nothing about that was cool or took any imagination.

He saw the kind of society that would come up with a Club 96 as the kind of society that needed a poke in the eye. We were not your 96 percent nor were we the hoodlums in the four percent. We were another category altogether — a category we defined for ourselves. We were the provocateurs, the irreverent ones. We'll crash your party, but we won't trash the place like the four percent would. No, we'll sneak in early, deflate the balloons, drink all the punch and hide the folding chairs in the boiler room.

I'd knock on Mack's door, and if there wasn't a plan afoot yet, they were re-living the last hijinks. And, just as likely, the mother — Mrs. Mack — was right in the middle of it.

Mrs. Mack — Catherine — was raising five kids on her own, her husband having died just before I came on the scene. He had left them a small life insurance policy and the house. She had a low-paying job — chambermaid at the motel just off the new highway on the edge of Dover. She was a hard-working, church-going woman, who insisted all her kids do well in school and go to college, which they did, a tribute to their native smarts and her determination. The sons became an insurance executive, an economist, a wildlife biologist and a developer and the one daughter head of a state agency.

But inside that stalwart woman of the working class was the same hellion that was inside Mack. She had the same complexion as my Irish father — so translucent it was ruddy from the veins in their faces. But where Dad's countenance was placid and stoic, hers twinkled with mischief. Fifty years after our gang had grown up and many had moved away, I got in touch with Mack and his youngest brother, Kevin, and we talked over coffee at Kevin's house in Dover.

I asked Mack to explain his mother, a mother not like any other mother in the neighborhood.

She and her siblings, Mack said, "grew up on a farm, and they got to do pretty much what they wanted. My mother, she wasn't very old when she got married, probably 21 or 22, and I think her attitude was: She's a widow with five kids and you can try to control five kids, but you probably can't and, as long as they are doing well in school and not getting in big trouble," then that was the best she could do.

"And I think the other thing on her mind is that things would come up that sounded like fun."

So when it came time to act on Mack's notion about Club 96, Mrs. Mack was the obvious choice to be the wheelman in the operation.

The radio station had been announcing all week that the winners of the Club 96 Halloween dance contest would win "the largest pumpkin ever grown in the state."

Since this was one of the few stations we could tune in on our car radios, we'd been hearing this announcement all week as we cruised around Dover with Mack driving his mother's 1957 green Plymouth. He had just gotten his license. The rest of us were a year or so younger.

The day before the dance, hearing the promise of the big pumpkin give-away one more time, Mack said, "That's what they think. We're going to take that pumpkin away from them right before their eyes."

When we got back to his house, Mack started to lay out the plan. It was like watching one of those World War II movies where there was a character to represent every stereotype in the American melting pot. The wise-crack-ing Brooklyn kid would be the first in the door of the Nazi headquarters. The slow-talking country boy had the arm for lobbing grenades. The Jewish guy would use his brains to distract the Germans. All directed by the skinny lieutenant who went to the Ivy League.

In Dover, there was not that much ethnic variety, but Mack — playing the part of the Ivy Leaguer — had a range of personalities and body types to choose from and as he began I realized what he chose for me would tell me a lot about who he thought I was. Since I wasn't so sure of that yet myself, I welcomed this assessment — unless he left me out or gave me an assignment that was the equivalent of playing right field.

"Ok, here's the deal," he said, as we gathered in the family's living room, a half dozen boys and two females: his 15-year-old sister and his 41-year-old mother. "We're going to distract the cops and the deejay and when they're not looking, we'll grab the pumpkin and run down the back stairs with it. My mother will be there with the car, and we'll get away before they know what happened.

"Except for my mother, we're all going to need to get into the dance and you need a Club 96 membership card to get in, so we're all going to go up to the station in a bit and get those cards," Mack said.

"Now, everyone will have a job to do: Cricket and Spence, you two start it off by going up to the deejay and get him looking away from the pumpkin."

Cricket was David Crockett and Spence was Tom Spencer. Cricket had been given his first name before "Davy Crockett, King of the Wild Frontier" had become the most popular show of the mid-Fifties. Cricket was the most all-American looking guy we had in the group — sandy hair, average build, a good baseball and basketball player and a smart kid.

Spence was the closest thing we had to a four-per-center in the group. He had his near-albino hair cut in a flattop when he was a boy and it stayed that way until the last time I saw him, when he was around 60. His slouch seemed to be saying to his teachers, "Hell, no, I will not stand up straight." He was the only one of us to smoke cigarettes; smoking was a sign of rebelling back then, but not our kind of rebelling. It was too obvious.

"Minnie and Boris," said Mack. "I want you two to start a fight in the lobby to distract the cop they have at the door."

Minnie was John Miniter. Boris was my nickname, after Boris Badanov, a portly and bumbling Russian spy on "The Rocky and Bullwinkle Show," a satirical cartoon featuring a talking moose which was one of our favorites.

Mack gave everyone names from the show. Mine was the only one that stuck. I didn't look at all like Boris Badanov. I was more gangly than stout, but I did have a slightly dark complexion and maybe it was the Armenian in me that prompted the nickname: Armenia at the time was part of the Soviet empire. But I liked it. "Boris"was exotic, off-beat and gave me an identity in the group that was distinct from my identity at home and in school.

"Okay, while you guys are distracting everyone, me and T-Bo will snatch the pumpkin and take it down to the back stairs. My mother and Barbara will be in the car and we'll all meet up back at my house," Mack said. T-Bo — Terry — was one of his younger brothers.

We'd picked up our membership cards already and all of us jammed into Mrs. Mack's Plymouth on a crisp October night, 1963. Seven or eight of us in one car? No problem — cars didn't have seat belts yet, as good a dividing line between the way things were and what they were soon to become. The world we occupied that night, the world where we did not worry about much, one where we lived in the now, would soon end.

Even as we were plotting this escapade, the president of South Vietnam, Ngo Dinh Diem, had just escaped a coup; J. Edgar Hoover was setting up a wiretap of Martin Luther King; and in a few weeks, President John F. Kennedy would be assassinated in Dallas. Harbingers, all of them, of a world we would soon be entering — a world with a war each of us would have to take part in or find a way to avoid; a world marred by racial prejudice, a fact we would not be able to ignore if we ended up leaving lily white New Hampshire; a world in political upheaval that would ask us to make a stand, right or left, liberal or conservative, involved or apathetic.

All of that — the blood pooling on the jungle floor in Vietnam and staining a pink dress in Texas and spilling onto a balcony in Memphis — was about to enter our consciousness. But that night we were just on a crazy lark. Like Dylan Thomas playing Indians, we were aware only of ourselves. Tonight, we were going to steal the biggest pumpkin in the state and rain on the parade of the 96 percent.

Dover City Hall was and still is an imposing brick-and-granite structure. The entrance was up a steep set of steps and past 25-foot granite columns. The clock tower and cupola were a brilliant white, topped by a golden dome. The interior was all deep, dark wood and cold stone floors. Our city hall echoed with authority. The perfect place to send our message.

When we walked up the stairs to the second floor auditorium, we could hear the deejay playing one of the most saccharine songs of the year, "Hey, Paula." The song begins, "Hey, hey Paula, I want to marry you."

Inside the girls wore modest shirtdresses or party dresses with petticoats, low heels and hair in flips. The boys wore pressed beige chinos, button-down shirts in checks or stripes. It's still a year or two away from the Beatles-inspired long hair; no boy wore his hair more than a few inches long. We all went to the barbershop once a week.

Mack had told us to wait until 8:30 to start the distraction. There was just one cop, and he wasn't anyone we knew. He was young and tall and did not look easy to trick. My breathing was getting quicker, and I felt like the cop was studying me.

"Minnie, is this gonna work? That cop is looking right at us."

"No he isn't, Boris. OK?"

I was worried. Will we get arrested? Will the cops call my parents? I wanted to belong, to be accepted, to be just as crazy as everyone else, but not if there was a consequence. That angelic boy in the catechism, that upright Boy Scout, that first-born of the new generation wanted to come up with an excuse to stop this thing right here.

That's when Minnie pushed me hard with both hands, nearly knocking me on my ass while he yelled, "Hey, jerk, are you looking at me!"

I was so shocked, I forgot this was just an act and got to my feet and tried to tackle Minnie and soon we were rolling around in the floor. Not exactly a fist-throwing fight, but enough of a scuffle to have the cop come over and tell us, "Cut it out! And get the hell out of here."

We got up and ran down the steps having caused a minute's distraction at best. But at least I hadn't chickened out, even if that was what I'd been trying to figure out a way to do.

Safely outside, we started walking to Mack's house, less than a mile away, when the green Plymouth went speeding by. Did they get the pumpkin? Mrs. Mack honked the horn and Barbara rolled down her window and whooped at us. Success!

Back at Mack's, everyone was quiet, listening to the radio broadcast from the dance. Twelve-year-old Kevin — Kev-Bo, as we called him, the youngest of the McEneaney brothers — was perched on the pumpkin, which was as big as a chair.

"Okay, we've got the winners of the dance contest," we heard the deejay say and he named Cindy, a girl from our neighborhood, a skinny blonde who would someday be famous in Dover for dating a second-rate major league baseball player, and her dance partner, a kid named Ricky who wore a bow tie and white bucks to school.

"These two young people are part of the 96 percent of the good kids and tonight they have won the biggest pumpkin in the state. It must weigh 50 pounds. I'm going to ask the stage crew to bring it to the mic so we can present it to Cindy and Ricky."

"Ahhh," the deejay said with a slow hesitation. "Ok, I guess we'll have to give that to you later. It was on the stage a little while ago."

We all started laughing and screaming and rolling on the living room floor.

The pumpkin was no longer just an oversized member of the squash family. Now, it was a story that would live on for years, repeated every Halloween, and among the players in the tale would be the one-time Prince of Wentworth Street.

Just up the street a quarter of a mile, my parents were ending their evening routine: The empty glass of Kruger, a residue of suds clinging to its side, sat in the sink; my mother's last lipstick-stained Pall Mall has been stubbed out in her ashtray. They did not know I had taken one more step away from them, away from being John Thomas Christie and towards being Boris.

The author, the surfboard and the Stingray,
owned by his friend and neighbor, Spence.

CHAPTER 17

A medal for Boris

Mack had a notion.

Well, he had lots of notions, but they would have been just the idle boast of a bored teenager if they had come from someone else, someone who didn't pull off just about every adventure he dreamed up.

His notions were coming to have a theme: freedom. The freedom of the open road, the freedom of the West Coast, the freedom from the staid tradition of the Northeast, the freedom to do what felt exciting even if you didn't have the wherewithal to pull it off.

No money to have our own private basketball court? A little ingenuity and a little larceny and problem solved.

No money for a boat, water skis and a place on a lake? Just take apart an old car, add a chain and a big field, and off we went.

The best expressions of freedom were coming from California around the time we were in high school, and we were devouring them all via television, magazine and the movies.

Movies like "Rebel Without a Cause" and books like "The Hells Angels" by a writer who would someday come to be as famous as the motorcycle gang he immortalized, Hunter S. Thompson. What was freer than the wind in your face astride a motorcycle?

But we didn't have a motorcycle, and we sure didn't have the hundreds of dollars it would take to buy even a beat-up used one.

But Mack had a notion.

He noticed that a motorcycle had been sitting for some weeks near the park where we played football.

"That's been there a long time, now," he said. "I think we can declare it abandoned."

The engine was bad, so we wheeled it up the street, hid it in his basement, and he replaced the engine with one he had somehow got his hands on without the passing of any money. Soon, we were all taking turns riding the unregistered bike up and down the back streets of Dover.

I had no idea how to ride a motorcycle and neither did anyone else. They just hopped on and figured it out, fishtailing, swerving, not stopping at stop signs because they didn't know how the brakes worked. This seemed like a bad idea to me, a recipe for broken bones or worse. But I had lived through Mack's other schemes, and when it was my turn, I didn't hesitate. I'd rather crash the damn thing and have to go to the hospital than be left out, be less of a guy than the rest of them.

What I remember the best was not fear, but the exhilaration of flying across the pavement, sensing to lean into the corners rather than steer, the torque from the engine riding right up my backside and into my arms as I twisted the accelerator.

I maneuvered the bike back to Mack's front yard, set the kickstand and slid off her like I had been riding motorcycles all my life.

Around that time, something even fresher was coming out of California, an intoxicating mix of music, cars and the beach. Rock 'n' roll spread from the confined studio of Dick Clark's "American Bandstand" in dreary Philadelphia to the beaches of southern California where the Beach Boys drove their T-Birds around dead man's curve with their arms around girls in bikinis.

We wanted some of that freedom.

We couldn't get a T-Bird, and the sexual freedom of the west coast was still some years away from New Hampshire. But, there, sticking out of the back of the T-bird or strapped to the top of the Beach Boys' woodie station wagon was an artifact of this freedom that Mack believed was within our reach.

A surfboard.

Mack thought we should become surfers.

There was one problem. Kids like us were surfing in California, but not in New England. Not yet. You couldn't even buy a surfboard anywhere near us, or within hundreds of miles.

Mack had another notion.

We'll make our own surfboards and teach ourselves to surf.

I said building a surfboard was a great idea because I thought every idea Mack had was great. But to myself I thought it will never happen because I, for one, couldn't make anything from scratch and, besides, all we knew about surfing came from a few photos in magazines and album covers. Sure, it looked like the very height of cool, the very definition of West Coast adventure. Although I doubt we said it out loud or even used the word in our minds, it was sexy. Surfers were handsome, athletic and daring, and they wore these long swim trunks decorated in multi-colored swirls. Just the type to attract a girl in a T-Bird.

I wasn't a bad swimmer and was — and still am — able to tolerate, even revel in, the cold water of New England beaches. But that wasn't going to be much help in balancing on a board on the top of a wave, even a small wave.

I expressed none of this. I didn't want to be called a scaredy cat.

The other guys passed on the idea, probably because, even though we all grew up less than 10 miles from the Maine and New Hampshire beaches, they were never up for swimming there: "Too damn cold, Boris. How the hell do you do it?"

The first problem was building the boards. Mack solved that in his usual confident way: He went to the library, thumbed through recent copies of Popular Mechanics and found plans for building your own surfboard. So that winter, we bought the materials — wood for the stringer down the middle and for the keel; Styrofoam to be shaped for the buoyant sides; and Fiberglas and resin to make a hard surface.

For weeks that winter we worked in Mack's basement, cutting the stringer with a jig saw, shaping the Styrofoam with a rasp, mixing the toxic-smelling resin in buckets.

I helped. A little. But Mack knew what he was doing or at least acted like he did, and by the time the snow was off the streets in the spring of '64, we had two surfboards.

The best beach for waves was Long Sands in York, Maine, the beach my parents took us to, the beach we went to as teenagers, a mile-long expanse of hard sand facing right on to the open Atlantic. The water there was always cold, so cold my parents would make me come out of the water after a half hour because my lips were turning purple, and I was starting to shiver. In July.

The finished boards lay across a set of saw horses in Mack's cramped and damp basement. Hard, sleek dolphin-like shapes, unpainted, so they were a dull yellow from the Fiberglas coating.

Nothing ever looked more like the future.

That surfboard, that was the next stage in my new life. If I could actually surf, actually get into that frigid water and imitate what I had seen on TV and in magazines and ride a wave, standing up on the thing like a Beach Boy, a California surfer, I would think pretty well of myself. I would have that thing I had been chasing since I left the good boy behind.

I'd have confidence.

Mack pointed out that even I, who could handle the chill waters of York Beach, should either wait 'til the weather got better or get a wetsuit. I didn't want to wait. I wanted to surf and surf in conditions that demonstrated that I, too, was a little crazy, a little wild.

So, I went to the local hardware store that also sold sports equipment. The wetsuits were beyond my budget, which was probably no more than $5 or so. But, on the sale table was a wetsuit jacket, no bottoms, and short-sleeved to boot. No diver wanted less than half a wet suit. Which is why I got it for the $5.

That winter I had turned 16 and gotten my driver's license. My aunt, Army Mae, bought a new car and gave me her 1957 Chevy, two-tone, yellow and white. I had a car and a surfboard, and I borrowed a roof rack, and on a sunny Saturday in April, with the temperature in the 50s, I tied the surfboard to the rack and drove to the beach alone. I didn't ask anyone to come along because if I failed, I didn't want a witness. If I succeeded, I'd have a story to tell. It didn't occur to me to worry about whether my pals would believe me if I told them I had surfed because even though we lifted a few things in our time, we didn't lie to each other.

In the summer, we'd have to get to the beach early to get one of the parking spots on Long Beach Avenue, but on that day I had my pick. A few people watched the surf from the comfort of their cars; no one was even walking the sand. In the car, I stripped down to my bathing shorts, slipped on the wetsuit jacket and carried the board down to the water's edge. The wind was modest, the waves about three feet, small compared to the photos I had seen from California, so I was more concerned about whether they would be big enough to propel me than worried that they'd knock me over.

Typically, the water temperature in southern Maine in April is about 40 degrees, only about eight degrees warmer than a bathtub filled with ice water. I walked into that cold water up to my ankles and walked right back to the sand. Unbearable. It felt like my toes would freeze and crack off like icicles. But the board lay ready on the sand; the surf was up. I was pretty sure I wasn't going to die, just be in pain.

I grabbed the board, carried it to the water, laid it down, draped myself across it like I had seen in the photos, arms hanging off the sides, and paddled out through the breakers. The foaming surf washed over my head and I just kept paddling until I was on the ocean side of the waves. I maneuvered the board to face the beach and turned my head to see the next wave coming in and tried to imitate what I had seen on TV — paddle furiously ahead of the incoming wave. Once I was in its trough and looked back, I realized that the waves I had seen from the street which had seemed so small were actually big and threatening. I put my head back and kept paddling, waiting for what was supposed to happen — feeling the wave take over with enough force that I could stop paddling and try to stand up and ride it in.

But the wave kept going and I didn't. I turned the board around and paddled out to try again. And again. Each time, the wave moved forward, leaving me stalled on its backside.

Except for what was covered by the wet suit top, my body was so cold you could have stuck me with a pin and I wouldn't have felt it. Between paddles, I was blowing on my hands to get some relief.

I got up on the board for a moment, then slipped off it, and both of us —man and board — washed up on the beach. But I had learned something — timing. Get my speed up and keep it up in the trough until I could sense the board was moving faster than I could paddle it. In that moment, when the wave had taken over, I could stand up and figure out what to do.

The next attempt worked, and I found myself erect on the board, shifting my weight to steer it away from the break so that I could ride it as far as possible. I looked across the tip of the board, saw the length of the beach where I was once a toddler playing in the sand and my dad protected his florid complexion under an umbrella, and my mother smoked and drank coffee from a thermos. And then I realized I had done it, I had surfed, I had conquered a wave and my fear and the cold.

Then the oomph went out of the wave, and I jumped off, dragged the board up to the car as fast as I could, tore off the wet suit jacket and jumped into the car, wet and shivering. I turned on the engine and ran the heat up high.

When I got back to Dover I told the story.

Mack had said I was crazy to even try. Now that I had tried and succeeded, had taken his notion and made it real, now there was no more doubt.

"Boris," he said, "you really are crazy."

It was a medal I wore proudly.

The gang at Mrs. Mack's home, Wallingford Street, Dover, N.H., circa 1970. Back row: Barbara (McEneaney) Mahoney; below her, "Mrs. Mack," Catherine McEneaney; Ed Sheehy (Mack's cousin) and his future wife, Wendy MacKenzie; Marty Mahoney. Second row: Chucky Mone; Marty Mahoney Jr.; Ray Hood; Kevin McEneaney; Mary Mone and daughter Coleen; bottom row: John "Minnie" Miniter; the author; James "Mack" McEneaney; Ginny Pinsince (later married to the author).

CHAPTER 18

Incident on Niles Street

Every kingdom needs a court jester.

The "Henry Law gang," as we were once referred to in the local newspaper's report on an event involving the dismantling and then re-mantling of a cranky neighbor's picket fence, had our own — a court jester with a good fool's name: Rube.

Even at age 13 or 14, Rube walked with an old man's bent-over stature and, on the rare occasion when he ran, it was more like a flailing of four limbs unacquainted with each other. He spoke fast, with a foamy lisp, his spittle all too visible. He tossed a ball like a girl, seemed unacquainted with hygiene of any sort and failed at school.

Rube's father was known as a demanding boss at a local shoe factory and was hard on his son, too. So, it was no surprise that Rube was desperate for attention from all of us, but especially from Mack, the "father" of the gang. Rube kept trying to win Mack's approval, perhaps because he knew he would never win his father's.

Rube would come giraffe-ing down the street, yelling from 50 yards away, "Mack! Mack!" and holding aloft his latest botched attempt at assembling a model car that left layers of dried glued still attached to his fingertips.

His father had a better-paying job than any of the other fathers, and his mother worked, too. Perhaps to help him be accepted, perhaps just to keep him out of their hair, Rube's parents slipped him dollars like our parents bestowed nickels and dimes. This meant Rube had more money than any of us, and he used it to try to buy status in the gang.

When the latest albums from one of our favorite groups came out — the Beach Boys, for example — Rube would rush to the store and buy it.

He'd show up at Mack's house or at the basketball court waving the shiny new album, and once he had us in his grip he'd have us marching down to his house to hear it. But once we got there, sometimes he would play it, other times just as it seemed he was about to play it or offer to sell it to you for pennies, he'd open the window in his room and sling the vinyl record into the field behind his house.

If he had a new model car kit to show off — we were all into model kits then — he might just as well take one of the plastic pieces in his hand, light it on fire and watch it melt onto his bedroom floor.

Was Rube allowed into the gang just so we could take advantage of him, get to hear the latest rock 'n' roll album, give him a dollar for a cherry skateboard he'd paid twenty bucks for, the change in our pockets for a model car still in its Revell box? Or was it simply the case that Mack — whose leadership and judgment we never questioned — was too generous and tolerant to blackball Rube, and the freebies were a happy but incidental benefit of Rube's admission?

The answer is probably much simpler: Rube's antics, annoying as they were sometimes, made the story of who we were more complete. Rube Wiggins had the one thing no one else in the gang possessed: a built-in homing device for finding a banana peel.

As much as he was our court jester, as much as he was unpredictable and destructive and sometimes even violent, Rube was still one of us. We never called him a "loser" or "" or even "slow," the terms we used back then for what we would now call a learning disability.

Our casual exploiting of Rube's longing for acceptance seemed almost harmless in those less sensitive times. We didn't force Rube to give us his stuff to be part of the gang. But even with his learning disability, he was savvy and needy enough to figure out that giving us stuff we couldn't afford made him a more valued member of the gang.

Underneath his neediness, however, anger smoldered.

Which is how I almost got arrested for attempted murder.

It all started one day when Spence told me that Rube had a couple of new model kits. "Let's go over to his house," Spence suggested. "You know he's not gonna use any of the spare parts, and he'll just give them to us or sell to us for almost nothing, maybe a nickel."

The car kits made by Revell or AMT sold for about $2 and came in cardboard boxes the size of a shoebox. Two dollars was a lot of money at a time when you could get a Coke for a dime. Rarely did I have more than a few coins in my pocket, and the same went for the rest of the gang. We'd get a model every few months by saving up money we'd get from little jobs or the dollar from a relative for a birthday, and we always asked for a model at Christmas.

The kits included not just the body, chassis, wheels and seats, but also the smaller parts, like steering wheels, bumpers, head- and taillights, rear view mirrors, antennas, perhaps a Continental Kit (the spare tire mounted inside a fancy cover on the rear bumper), or side exhaust pipes for a hot rod. These smaller parts were attached to plastic trees and could be removed by gently twisting them off.

Rube didn't really want any of the albums or models he bought. He was more likely to sail the albums out his back window or set them afire or do a slipshod job of gluing together a model just for the purpose of blowing it up with a cherry bomb. He knew we couldn't afford these things and that was his brand of cruelty towards us — which I suppose we deserved.

It was also his way of getting our attention, because we would always try to "rescue" the album or model from him before he destroyed them or threw them away. So, when Spence heard Rube had made a fresh purchase, he moved quickly.

Rube lived in a two-story house at the end of Niles Street, a dead end street off Henry Law Avenue, not far from the Macks' house. When we got there, we found him sitting on his bed, going through parts of a model '56 Corvette, the one with the deep scoops behind the front wheels.

Spence, the budding punk among us, always treated Rube with disdain, which made Rube all the more susceptible to the rare display of friendship Spence showed on this day.

"Rube, what ya got there? Oh man, is that the 'Vette Revell just came out with? Cool. Can I take a look?"

"Yeah, I just got it. Look, Spence," Rube said, proudly handing over the opened box.

"Rube, you gonna use all these spare parts on the Vette? Ya got a lot here," Spence said.

"Spence, Spence, look at this, too." Rube was excited for the attention. "I got a whole box of that stuff."

He pulled an old model box from under his bed, jammed with a jumble of plastic trees, each one with three or four parts still attached.

Spence picked up one of the trees and handed another to me. He twisted off four chromed baby moon hub caps and dropped them into his shirt pocket, tossed that tree aside and picked up another one, a smaller, red plastic tree holding a set of bullet taillights and took those, too.

"Neat stuff, ain't they, Spence," Rube said.

"Yeah, I'm gonna reverse the rim on the '50 Ford I'm making and put the baby moons on them," Spence said.

I followed Spence's lead and took a tree with four chromed spoke wheels that would make the T-Bird I was customizing look even sharper.

Rube was always giving away things when he was in a good mood.

On this day, Spence's phony friendliness seemed to have put Rube in a particularly expansive mood. He never told us we could take those spare parts, but he didn't stop us, and after we had scavenged the parts we wanted and then some, we left.

But what we hadn't taken into consideration was Rube's mercurial personality. Except when Mack was around, Rube could go in a flash from an awkward and needy teenager to a spittle-spewing madman.

Spence and I were 50 yards down Niles Street, our pockets stuffed with Rube's unwanted bits of shiny plastic, when we heard him yelling, "Spence! Boris! You bastards!"

Just as we turned to look back, we heard rocks hitting the pavement. Rube was giraffe-ing down the street, picking up rocks from the shoulder and flinging handfuls our way.

One hit me in the back of the leg, doing no harm. I picked it up and threw it back at him and was about to take off running when I saw Spence hefting a softball-sized rock. Rube was still chasing us, still screaming "bastards" in his lisp — "bath-tuurds" — and I swear he was foaming at the mouth.

"I'm not gonna take this from Rube," Spence declared and heaved the stone into the air. It came down directly on Rube's head, and he went down like Goliath.

Spence took off, and I took off after him.

"He started it," Spence said as we ran up Henry Law Avenue and that was all he needed — and all I needed — to put Rube out of our minds. The nut was trying to kill us. Our consciences were clear.

Then.

But mine isn't now. Not until I wrote this and visualized that pathetic, gawky kid collapsing, a hand to his head, did I admit to myself that leaving him in the street, just because I was scared of getting into trouble, was an act of sheer cowardice. My first big chance at putting into practice the ethos of the Catechism and the Boy Scout Handbook, I turned and ran home.

When I came into the kitchen, my father noticed I was out of breath.

"Did you run all the way up the street?"

"Yeah. Spence and me were running away from Rube. He was throwing rocks at us. He's crazy."

I left it at that and was on my way to my room with my model parts when I saw out of the picture window a police cruiser pull into our driveway and another one pull into Spence's. There could be no other reason there were cruisers at both houses unless it was about Rube.

I saw a police officer get out of his car, take his nightstick from the seat and slide it into his belt. The wooden stock of his handgun stood out brown against the blue uniform. A heavy, forceful knock on the door, which my father opened. My breathing was no longer automatic. I had to force myself to inhale and exhale.

"Is John Christie your son? Is he here?"

I walked into the kitchen, the policeman looked at me and said, "You have to come with me down to the station. That boy, the one you threw rocks at, he's hurt bad. He's at the hospital. He might not make it."

My father turned to me, not angry, it seemed, but shocked, as was I. He didn't say a thing. There was just that look when the shock passed, the look I realized when I became a dad myself that every father needs: Call it the hairy eyeball. The eyes narrow, the mouth sets, the brow furrows. If you employ it sparingly, if your kid believes you have moral authority, if you never threaten and never hit, then the stare-of-death is all you'll ever need to scare a kid into doing the right thing.

I wasn't going to throw rocks again at anything, never mind another kid. But, first, I had to be arrested.

The policeman told my father he could drive me down to the station himself, but we needed to go immediately. During the trip there I told him, my voice shaking, what had happened, emphasizing that it was Spence, not me, who had sent Rube to the hospital.

My dad was a man of few words and that day was no exception. "What are you doing throwing rocks at all? I don't care if Rube started it, you boys could have outrun him. I don't know what's going to happen, but you are going to tell the truth and take the consequences," he said, turning his face towards me, his expression utterly impassive, showing neither anger nor sympathy. He was coming with me to the station, but I was on my own once we got there. That was the message.

The Dover police station was in the basement of city hall. When we arrived Spence and his dad were already in the station. We sat next to them on the bench where they were waiting, and just then Rube's dad burst into the room.

His sport shirt was hanging half un-tucked from his trousers, his dark hair was on end as if he had run his hand through it over and over again. He came right up to us, fists clenched, his arms moving up and down in a pounding motion and bawled, "You killed my boy! He's up in the emergency room! His head's bashed in! He's not gonna make it! How could you do this!"

I had no idea how to respond but when my dad pushed me off the bench I quickly got the idea. "I'm sorry, Mr. Wiggins. We didn't mean to hurt him," I said. I wanted to add that Rube started it, but I could feel the hairy eyeball burning a hole in the back of my shirt so I just looked down at the floor.

The officer who had come to my house intervened just then and told us it looked like Rube was hurt so bad that we could be charged with attempted murder. "Or worse, if he doesn't make it. So you boys ought to sit there thinking about what you did."

What I was thinking about was reform school. I imagined myself in a dreary brick building with rows of metal bunk beds, dressed in gray work clothes, eating meals of watery oatmeal. I hated oatmeal. And getting into fights every day because that's the kind of boys who get sent away to reform school.

When I finally looked up from the floor and had begun to accept my fate, I saw that Mr. Wiggins had left. One of the officers called the two dads over and they nodded their heads at whatever the officer was telling them.

"Okay, Mr. Christie and Mr. Spencer" — meaning me and Spence, not our fathers — "come on over here. I want to show you something," the officer said. "Quick. Get up now!"

I stood up straight and stiff, nearly shivering from fright.

He opened the wooden gate on the low bar that separated the public area from the rest of the station and led us down a damp hallway to what he wanted us to see.

"See those two cells? That's where I'm going to put you two until we figure out what to charge you with. Go in there, I want you to see what it feels like."

I moved swiftly into one cell and Spence the other. Then the officer closed the doors, locked them and walked away, leaving us sitting on narrow beds with thin mattresses, looking between the bars at a bare granite wall, the foundation of city hall. We sat on those hard bunks, staring at the iron bars in terror for what seemed like an eternity but was probably no more than 10 minutes until the police officer returned. He opened the doors and told us we could go home while they continued investigating and figured out what punishment was warranted.

The ride home with Dad was silent. He smoked, I looked out the window and tried to stop myself from thinking about having to face my mother. Tried but failed, so that by the time we finished the five-minute drive from the police station to our house, I was almost overwhelmed by dread. I seemed to be more worried about what my mother would do to me than about what the police would do.

"Wait outside for a minute, John," my father said. "I want to talk to your mother first."

After a few minutes, Dad stuck his head out the door and told me to go straight to bed. My mother was sitting in the living room, smoking her Pall Malls, violently tapping her foot as only she could do, her back to me while I hastened up the stairs to the bedroom I shared with Gary.

I don't know what Dad said to her. But the fact that she kept her back to me told me everything about how she'd responded. Her refusal even to look at me was much worse than the diatribe I was expecting. This was clearly a crime too serious for the usual loud and hysterical "Jesus, Mary and Josephs" that met even my most minor misdemeanors.

The next morning when I got to school, half expecting that the cops would show up later that day to arrest me for murder, Mack's brother T-Bo told me he had just seen Rube.

"What? Where? I thought he was still in the hospital," I said.

"No. He was walking down the street to school," T-Bo said. "He did have a Band-Aid on his head, though."

It took me awhile to figure it all out. But eventually I realized that Spence and I had been fooled by a ruse executed by our fathers and the cops at the police station. At some point, while Spence and I were wallowing in our fear, the cops got word that Rube was barely hurt. When they shared that with our fathers the four men hatched a plan to keep that news to themselves and throw us into the cells to teach us a lesson. Letting us go home afterwards, to spend the night in terror of what was to come and remorse over what we had done, would drive the lesson home further.

I can't say what it did to Spence, but I can certainly vouch for the fact that it worked on me. That and the hairy eyeball from my father were all I needed to understand the gravity of what we had done — or nearly done, anyway.

This was the first time that any of my antics with Mack's gang led to anything serious. And it was the last. It also showed me a side of my father I hadn't seen before. The only other time I had occasion to see that kind of steely disapproval came a couple of years later when — fully apart from anything involving Mack and the gang — I tried to pull a fast one on some boys.

Me and Gary with dad. I'm 16, Gary is 13.

CHAPTER 19

Caught stealing

Lying was so forbidden by my father that I pictured it as a circle of throbbing red light, a fearful and shameful miasma from which there was no emerging as innocent as you went in. This fear came from my father, but also from my mother, the Baltimore Catechism, the Ten Commandments, the red-faced nuns, the image of Christ dying on the crucifix that was in all our classrooms, and the framed print of Jesus and his bleeding heart that hung in every Catholic home.

When I hit driving age, an event happened that resulted in my receiving the ultimate lesson in honesty from my father. I had nearly wrecked the transmission in the used Chevy my Army Mae gave me when I was a high school senior by peeling out over and over. By that fall, I needed a more reliable car to go from home to the University of New Hampshire campus, about five miles away. I babied the Chevy well enough to get it to a nearby dealership and that's when I saw her.

She was British. A two-seater roadster. Not a Jag or even an MG, but something even smaller: a red Austin-Healy Sprite, about three years old, the little brother to the more established Austin-Healy 3000.

It was just a bit bigger than a go-kart. It was called a bug-eye for the teardrop headlights pressed into the hood. The car was so stripped-down basic that it didn't even have side windows — just two bolted-on clear plastic screens that could not be rolled down. They were either on or off.

The salesman let me try it out. It was unlike anything I had driven before. There was no slack in the steering: Turn it an inch and the thing went right where you pointed it. It was low and quick and took curves and corners without heeling over at all unless you really pushed it. It was cool. It was British. It was a goddamn sports car, and it was as impractical as a motor scooter for getting around during the long New England winters.

For the Chevy and $200, I had myself a little red roadster, and I was soon putting that Sprite through its paces, top down and feeling as sure of myself as I ever had.

It was fun, fun, fun — and a mechanical mess. The electrical system caught fire regularly. It burned so much oil, I kept a five-gallon can of heavy-weight oil in the trunk so I could lubricate the engine on demand. One day, going up a hill, it just stopped dead. The mechanic said I had likely broken the rear axle. I didn't have the money to fix it. I was stuck.

Some guys a little older than me were hanging around the garage.

"Love the car," one of them said. "How's it run? Is it for sale?"

"Runs good. Burns a little oil," I said, not mentioning the bad axle and, apparently, they didn't know why the Sprite was in the garage, so I added, "Just getting a little tune up."

"Would you take $250 for it right now?"

"Sure," I said, relieved that with $250 and maybe a little more I could find another used car and not have to fix this one.

They gave me the cash, and I thumbed my way home.

"Where's that little car?" Dad asked me. "What was wrong with it?"

"The guy there said I probably broke the rear axle."

"Jesus Christ, what's that gonna cost?"

"It was going to be quite a bit. That why I sold it. Got two-fifty for it."

I figured this was good news. Got rid of a damaged car that I couldn't afford to repair and had all that money in my wallet.

"Well, who paid that much for a car with a broken axle?"

"Some older guys that were hanging out at the garage."

"And they knew it needed an expensive repair?"

"No. I didn't say anything about that."

Dad's red face, the Irish face of visible arteries and veins, turned redder.

"What are you talking about? You sold them a car that doesn't run? You lied to those boys. I'm ashamed of you. You have to find them and give them their money back."

I didn't have to find them. When they tried to drive away after I had left the garage, they found out what I had done and they found me.

They still wanted the car, but they wanted $200 of the $250 back. I ended up with $50, no car, a rare angry father and a shame that I can feel to this day.

John W. Christie, my dad's older brother, who was killed in France during the last days of World War I.

CHAPTER 20

The boy and the casket

One summer day when I was in my late teens, my father did something he had never done before. He brought a friend home from work.

It just wasn't something he did. The only people who ever came to our home were uncles, aunts, cousins and the occasional neighbor.

We were not social people.

Just as surprising — more surprising — was the man he brought home: the janitor at Eastern Air Devices, where dad was a machinist and union officer. The black janitor. Or, as my parents would have said, the colored janitor.

Bill was a thin and compact man of about 40, dressed in a heavy blue work shirt. His faced was well-creased, and I remember being struck how the whites of his eyes seemed almost tan.

My father offered his usual chair at the kitchen table to Bill, and my mother served them coffee.

I sat in my usual chair, too, stunned, fascinated and puzzled. They talked about work, I presume. The conversation didn't interest me — but I could

109

not stop looking at Bill. I had seen pictures of black people in magazines and on our black-and-white TV, but I had hardly ever seen a black person in — well — in person.

The population of Dover at the time was about 15,000 and, according to the census of 1960, the city was 99.9 percent white, meaning the non-white population was about 15 people. Even that seems like a lot, because if there were even as many as 15 people of color in the city, they were well hidden, unless it was the family that ran the one Chinese restaurant.

In Dover, "diversity" — a word I didn't hear commonly used for another 25 years — was comprised of various white ethnic groups: Irish, French-Canadian, a few Greeks and Syrians, the Scotch-English (aka WASPs), not many Italians and a tiny Jewish population of Eastern European ancestry.

I didn't ask any questions then, but years later I asked my mother what prompted Dad to invite the black co-worker home.

"Your dad felt sorry for him," she said. "He was a hard worker at the shop, but he didn't have any friends there so your dad just thought it would be a nice thing to do."

It wasn't a grand gesture. I never heard my parents discussing politics or the civil rights movement. But they knew right from wrong and how to treat people, and that's where their politics and social conscience began and ended.

Yet, that little incident stayed with me always. As I probed the questions of this story — Who made me? Why am I the way I am? — I wanted to know why my father seemed to have a level of empathy so deep he would risk the disapproval of his fellow workers by befriending a man some of them likely called the slur of the period.

Somewhere in his past my father had acquired a sensitivity that I was too young to ask about when he was alive, but as an adult I might have taken greater notice of those watery eyes and his air of quiet resignation. I might have had a beer with him. I might have asked him about his life, his past — and he might have told me about that day in 1918 that must have filled him with a sadness that played a big part in who he became. And, as his son, in who I became.

• • •

Every few weeks, my father would bring my brother and me to his mother's apartment. She lived in a two-family Victorian house on the lower end of Belknap Street in a section of town going downhill from solid working class to run down.

Befitting the cliché of the proper Irish Catholic household, the bay window was hung with lace curtains. A small vertical banner hung by the door, a gold star against a panel of white, bordered in red. I always noticed it, but never asked what it was and didn't learn its meaning until I looked deeper into my Dad's past.

The tiny living room spoke "grandmother" — heavy overstuffed chairs and a love seat in browns and dark blues, little tea tables covered in white doilies and a stale smell of yesterday's cabbage and boiled potatoes. A picture of Christ's vivid bleeding heart was hung in one room; a small plaster statue of the Blessed Virgin in her blue-and-white veil stood on a wooden shelf.

"Ma," as my father called her, let us go to her "ice box" for a Coke. The sweet drink helped us bear the interminable hour that my father sat here doing his duty to his mother, who seemed to us to be 100 years old.

I passed the time sipping the Coke and fixating on one photo hanging in the living room.

A large oval frame dominated one wall. It held a photo of my father's older brother and my namesake: John W. Christie. He was a doughboy, a soldier in the First World War, and the picture shows him in his khaki uniform. To me, at age eight or 10 or 12, it was the only interesting thing in the room, and I could fantasize about the uncle I would never know because he had died 30 years before I was born.

The story was thin back then, but I knew this much: Private John W. Christie was the first Dover man killed in combat in the First World War. There was a memorial to him on a traffic island next to the old Christie home on Locust Street, a brass plaque set into a boulder. In his honor as the first local death in the war, the city's American Legion Post was named after him.

And I knew — or did I imagine it? — that he had been shot by a German sniper as he was delivering a message from one officer to another. And I also had been told he had been a good baseball player.

From those skimpy facts, I had developed a fantasy of my Uncle John that allowed me to see myself inheriting his athletic prowess, his battlefield bravery and his leadership among the boys of Dover.

I pictured my uncle as a fleet base runner whose speed was noted in basic training. Radios were rudimentary and unreliable in the First World War, so they had to fall back on the oldest form of communication on the battlefield: Send a runner. As the fastest in his company, Uncle John was the one they sent.

I saw Private Christie in his khaki jacket, jodhpur pants, spats and dishpan helmet, dashing through the French woods, banking around tree roots, his leather boots throwing up bits of the forest floor in a land far away from the peaceful baseball fields of Dover. Suddenly there was the flash of a German rifle coming from behind a tree. Then the soldier in khaki – more a boy than a man — is struck in the back, flies forward and takes his last breath.

And from that time until I was well into my 60s, that was all I knew. I hoped if I could find out more about my Uncle John I might also find about Uncle John's little brother — my father.

• • •

My cousin Doug, son of my dad's sister Peg, was the only living Christie relative old enough to perhaps know something of Uncle John.

On a fall day in 2006, I drove the two hours from my home in central Maine to Dover, to Doug's little Cape on Wedgwood Road, a place I hadn't visited in more than 20 years. Doug was in his 70s, a retired insurance salesman, a tall man with a ruddy complexion, a fleshy baby face and a head of wavy hair. He looked more like my dad than I do. He greeted me in blue sweat pants and a loose sweatshirt, and we sat down at his dining room table over instant coffee.

"This is my work space now," Doug said, pushing aside a clutter of mail, papers and household items — a napkin holder, a paperweight, a screwdriver. Next to him lay a flattened Footjoy golf shoebox sealed with tape.

"I found this picture," he said, and pushed the cardboard sleeve to me.

I slid out the now-unframed sepia-toned photo of John W. Christie that had hung in our grandmother's living room. I had not seen it in at least 50 years.

The photo was nearly 90 years old and showing its age and treatment: crack lines led across his tunic and the background. Doug had taped them to keep them from getting worse. Someone had attached a one-inch square of khaki fabric over the right breast pocket; it was frayed on the edges like it had been there for years. I took it to be a piece of Private Christie's actual uniform. Doug agreed but didn't know who put it there or when — he, too, was born well after Uncle John had died in the war. Perhaps John's parents, whom everyone called Ma and Pa Christie, had kept and displayed it because it was once next to his flesh, to a body they would never hold again. That rough piece of fabric was all that was left of their first-born boy, who only months earlier they had hugged and kissed for what was to be the last time.

When I had a moment to really look at the photo, I no longer saw John as the dashing hero I'd fantasized about in my grandmother's parlor. Now, I saw him as what he really must have been: a young man, son of Irish immigrants, who had been put into a uniform and sent overseas to fight a futile war over ancient European rivalries that had nothing to do with his own life but had resulted in his death.

Doug was talking, but I was falling deeper into that face in the photo, the narrow eyes, the inverted eyebrows, the small, pouty lips, the oversized ears sticking out like fans and the acre of forehead below the wavy hair.

I knew an older version of that face — it was the face of Thomas Henry Christie, who 30 years after that portrait was taken would become "Dad" to me.

I wanted to weep.

When I went to visit Doug, my father had been dead for nearly four decades, and I thought I was well past mourning and sadness.

But the photo was a bridge to the past. It provided me with a way to truly feel a loss that I had been too self-involved to mourn when it happened. All I had to do was to let myself take those backward steps.

Doug got my attention again when he offered me a small manila envelope.

The first thing I saw in the envelope was a piece of blue-lined loose-leaf paper on which Doug had written down the inscription of Uncle John's gravestone:

John W Christie

NH

Pvt. 1 CL

325INF 82 Div

October 13, 1918

Born 1895

Deeper in the envelope were a few tiny black-and-white snapshots. Three were of the stone monument dedicated to Uncle John in Dover, fuzzy shots with a glossy finish and those crinkly-cut edges.

The other three were of an older style, a matte finish, 2½ by 4½ inches.

"I think these were taken at St. Mary Cemetery," Doug said. "You can keep them."

I studied them and surmised that they had been taken at Uncle John's burial in that Catholic cemetery set amid Dover farmland. By the 1960s, the area had been developed. There was a Ford dealership across from the cemetery where Mack and I and others climbed over the fence when the dealership was closed so we would be the first boys in town to see the hot new car of 1963, the Ford Mustang. And just up the street was the A&W root beer drive-in where I had nearly killed myself doing a wheelie on Spence's Bultaco motorcycle.

I realized now how many times I had been within yards of the dust-to-dust resting place of my namesake. I had never known he was buried there, never even bothered to ask my dad to take me to the grave of his brother, whom he had loved enough to give his name to his first-born son.

The first photo from the trio of cemetery pictures presented a confusing image. The top half was all washed out sky and the bottom was what appeared to be a parade float, the kind decorated with flowers. But then I looked closer and saw that these were flower arrangements; one was in the shape of a cross — the sort friends and family send to a funeral or burial.

The second picture depicted a man and two women, all dressed formally in black, the women displaying white bows or blouses under their jackets and wearing go-to-church hats. They are walking along a grassy path and in the background, very small because the photographer is far away, you can see the white convertible roof of a period car and behind it a wagon carrying a casket. Behind the wagon was a procession of men in uniforms.

I assume the trio is my grandparents and perhaps their oldest daughter.

The third photo is higher quality, taken in a better light and a little closer to the action. It confirms what I concluded from the second photo. Now, I can see that the wagon carries a flag-draped casket. I can count the stars on most of the visible rows of the flag: eight stars per row, making it a 48-star flag, accurate for circa 1918.

A khaki-clad soldier holds the reins of the team of four horses pulling the wagon, known as a caisson. An honor guard of sailors in their white caps appears to be standing at the grave, just ahead of the caisson, with civilians around them. Three soldiers march by the side of the caisson, and in their midst there is a boy in a white shirt. A few men in dark suits walk behind them. There are no dates written on the backs of the photos, but the fact that no one is wearing a coat and that the grasses are high and the elm trees still show all their leaves suggests the time is anywhere from late spring to early fall.

(Later, when I researched the local newspapers from the period, I discovered that the burial was in September, 1921, three years after the war, when the bodies of tens of thousands of American dead, including my uncle's, were disinterred from graves in France and sent home to their families.)

Doug agrees with my hunch that the trio must have been John's parents and probably one of his sisters. But we don't discuss the boy in the white shirt. I've taken special notice of him, and I think I know — or at least sense — who it is. But I say nothing about him while I'm at Doug's. I want to look more closely at him when I have more time and privacy.

I want to be alone with this photo.

I left the photos in their envelope for a few days after getting home, preparing myself to "read" the third photo for more than its frozen moment, to see it as a story — in particular about that boy. He is the only child in any of the photos.

When I finally decide I'm ready to look, I take out a magnifying glass and see that the boy is striding alongside the caisson, just a foot or two from the lead soldier. His head is facing towards the caisson and upwards, his stride long and determined. He is wearing dark knickers and knee socks. Assuming the soldier he is next to is of average height for the time, perhaps 5-foot-9, the boy appears to be five-feet tall, making him around 12–14 years old.

To get an even closer look, I use my photo editor's loupe — a strong magnifier I used to edit photo contact sheets when I worked at newspapers. You place it directly on the photo and put your eye to the top of the glass.

It reveals one new detail when I magnify the boy's head.

The back of his head is to the camera, and the light coming over the photographer's shoulder illuminates the back of the boy's ears.

They are big and protruding.

All the evidence adds up to what I felt when I saw the photo on Doug's dining room table: The boy sporting those ears is little Tommy Christie. He would have been 14 at the time of the burial.

The boy is the little brother of the dead man in the casket.

The boy is my dad.

The boy has just a few more minutes to be near his big brother before a bugler in uniform plays Taps and the casket is lowered into the ground.

I speculate that perhaps it was this day, this moment, that put the sadness in my dad's eyes and the empathy in his heart. The protective shield in which he enveloped my brother and me might have been his way of trying to ensure we did not have to experience anything harsh in our lives as he did at a tender age.

I look again and again at that photo and try to put myself in those knickers and hear the rim of the big wooden wagon wheels scraping and squealing on the metal axle. I sense the heat waves coming off the horses that are taller than the soldiers, feel the muscles in my neck strain to look up at the casket.

And I wonder what I would be feeling. What was Tommy Christie feeling?

I wish he had lived long enough that I could have looked at this photo with him and asked him. Being the quiet man he was, he might have said little or nothing, but I still would have known so much more about him even if the only response had been the look on his face.

• • •

After multiple trips to the Dover Public Library, searching through microfilm and some dusty clipbooks in the research room, I pieced together more of Uncle John's story.

I found the most telling piece of evidence in news stories published by the local newspaper, Foster's Daily Democrat. One story was dated Nov. 11, 1918, the last day of what was then called The Great War.

The story reported that two days earlier, my paternal grandmother, Elizabeth Christie, received a telegram from the War Department that began with those telltale lines that need no explanation, "We regret to inform you …"

Her son, 19-years-old, had been killed in action on Oct. 15, almost precisely one year after he was inducted into the Army. He had trained for seven months at a Georgia boot camp, becoming so good at riflery that he was made an instructor. In April, 1918, with the war still raging in the fields and forests of France and Germany, he was sent to England, where he was one of the thousands of American and British troops who marched in review before King George. It had been only a generation earlier that his Irish father had fled his country along with tens of thousands of his countrymen to escape the yoke of the English monarchs that ruled Ireland.

The story mentioned that Private Christie wrote two letters home, one about when he first saw action, on July 4, and another on Sept. 15 when he told his sister he was fighting on the front lines. Another news story confirmed what I recalled hearing as a boy: He had just returned from delivering a message to his captain and "was turning away when he was felled by a rifle bullet" fired by a German sniper. He died instantly in the Argonne forest, site of some of the bloodiest and most futile battles of what was called then the war to end all wars.

Had the war ended just a few weeks earlier, John W. Christie would have lived. The cruel irony of this bad timing reminded me of something I'd learned from the Tammy tape — that another brother in my family had also died just weeks before the end of that war. Moses Hovsepian, Nana's little brother, died not of a bullet but of starvation from a war waged by Germany's ally, Turkey. Though there is no record of the precise date of Moses's death, it was almost certainly within days or a few weeks of my father's brother's death.

Listening to Nana talk about Moses on that tape, I heard this most stalwart of women weeping, as she imagined that little boy eating grass when she could have fed him. Strong as she was, the memory of his death clearly never left her and made her heart ache for decades and decades.

Why, then, would my father's heart not also ache even 30, 40, 50 years after his brother died? I never saw him cry, never heard him speak of the death. But every time he visited his mother, he passed by that gold star banner hanging on her front door, the emblem, I learned later, given to every mother who lost a son in World War I.

All those Sunday afternoons while I nursed my bottle of Coca-Cola, my father and his mother often just sat silently in the presence of the ghost in the oval frame.

My mother's graduation picture from Dover High School, 1941.

CHAPTER 21

The best years of her life

In 1941, my mother graduated from high school, got a job at the woolen mill in Dover and finally had some freedom and some money, which it seems she spent on being fashionable. No longer the hand-me-down sweater set she wore for her high school graduation picture, turned front to back to hide a hole. Now, as I saw in a snapshot when she appears about 20 year old, she and a girlfriend pose on City Hall steps, each in dark two-piece dresses, with white bows adorning their coiffures. My mother had her skirt pulled just above her knees, her hands poised ladylike on her lap. She points her face upwards, her eyes are shining — the picture of optimism.

A few years later, in 1946, she was married and from then to 1968 were likely the best years of my mother's life. Not easy years — she worked a factory job all through that time while raising my brother and me and keeping a home for Dad and us. She also had some serious health problems– especially from that car accident — but she lived a safe, secure working-class life and eventually moved into her own, almost-new house. She was no longer the unwilling mother to five children, her siblings; now she was the wife of a solid working man she'd chosen to marry and mother to two boys, three years apart.

As Mrs. Thomas Christie, she gave cookouts at the Henry Law Avenue house and hosted the annual family Christmas dinners, where she laughed about always forgetting the rolls in the oven. One evening a week she took craft courses at the university; I still have the ceramic stuffed celery dish she made.

Not all was well. She had a short temper; she complained about her siblings relying on her too much to care for Nana; Gary got terrible grades most years.

Her work was demanding. She was one of the first employees hired at the new General Electric plant in nearby Somersworth, where they made electric meters. For many years, she sat on the assembly line constructing one piece of each meter that went by, using an electric soldering gun and lengths of lead wire. When the solder was heated, it melted and let off lead fumes. Even someone skilled at the job would occasionally burn a finger, as my mother did — I recall the burn marks on her hands. She likely had one of her Pall Malls going next to her while she soldered, inhaling the smoke from both the lead and the tobacco that would eventually kill her.

The fashionable dresses and heels would come out for holidays and graduations, but her day-to-day outfit at GE was a starched, cotton uniform dress.

I suspect she was a good worker because at some point in her time at GE they promoted her to inspector. She didn't have to make the meters any longer, just make sure they were made right.

At home, she was mostly focused on what she had to get done: A simple dinner, cleanup, then coffee and a cigarette or two while she read her Life or Look magazine. She made sure Gary and I did our homework. On the weekends, she did the grocery shopping, baked cupcakes for us and cleaned the house. Sometimes she came home from Harvey's bakery with fancy cupcakes or from Montgomery Ward's candy counter with my favorite, chocolate-covered peanuts.

On Sunday, while Dad took us to Mass, she'd make a nicer meal — ham, scalloped potatoes, green beans. In the good weather, my extended family went to a park or the beach, and my mother, her sister Mary and Nana would grill shish kebab, bringing along a pot of pilaf and stacks of Syrian bread. The men — Dad, Mary's husband, Art, and Uncle Licky — would smoke cigarettes and listen to the Red Sox on a car radio, while Gary and I tossed around a baseball.

My mother's demeanor at home was all-business, punctuated by occasional outbursts of anger and resentment, biting her fist to control what she might say. What did she get angry about? I don't remember anything in particular.

I do vaguely recall that she used to yell at me about my grammar school papers. Mine were always sloppy, as I had no interest in making them look neat once I was satisfied that I'd done the basic work. But the nuns required that the essays we wrote at home be handed in with a construction paper cover. The title of the essay had to be written in colorful script on the cover, which also had to be decorated with tiny colored stars glued around the edges.

I took about 30 seconds to make the cover because I didn't see the point of a pretty presentation. My mother would make me do it over because she knew that my haste and sloppiness would lose me a grade. But even on a second attempt I couldn't get the little stars lined up properly along a neat border. After two tries, however, she was too worn out to keep yelling, and she'd give in and let me hand in the essay as it was. Then, as she predicted, I'd get a "B" instead of the "A" I thought I deserved, and the comment written in red by the nun: "Neatness counts!"

There were rarely any marital disputes. I can only remember one. My father was not a big drinker, and never anything but his nightly beer, which he drank at home. The only night that, to my knowledge, he ever went to a bar, however, he drank whiskey and came home uncharacteristically jovial, singing and laughing with an uninhibited smile on his face I never saw before or after. (This is pretty much the way I react after too many bourbons.) It scared my mother — perhaps because she'd seen too many Irish drunks in Dover — and I remember her losing that famous temper and yelling at him to go to bed and sleep it off.

Dad was otherwise the man my mother could always count on, the man she loved and her family did, too. (Aunt Lity recalled that when she was home from nursing school my dad would slip her the occasional five-dollar bill.) To all of them he was "Tommy," Mr. Easy Going, the Irishman who never missed a day of work, smoked his Luckies, had a single glass of beer after dinner and called his wife, "Babe."

My mother may have been domineering with her family and friends and to some extent with me and Gary, but looking back I don't recall her ever telling Dad what to do — or him telling her. It was a quiet partnership with mostly traditional roles. She cooked and cleaned; he did the house repairs, mowed the lawn and shoveled the driveway.

Both of them did their part at seeing to it that their children behaved themselves. She exercised her authority by yelling. He exercised his through restraint. He had the kind of quiet strength that boys respond well to. I didn't need a lot of discipline to do what I was supposed to do in those early years — get passing grades, play on baseball and basketball teams, get to school on time, take care of my few possessions like a bike and a baseball glove. And later when I rebelled it was a pretty harmless form of rebellion. Nothing to cause much alarm, even if my parents had known about it, which for the most part they didn't.

Gary, though, was, as Army Mae said, "different." He was hard to wake in time to get to school, received more bad grades than good and was always late with his homework. He over-ate, would rather watch TV with Dad than play outside and had few friends. But none of these problems were big ones because our father was always there to give him a talking to and keep him in line. Dad was the kind of man — decent, hard-working, taciturn, war veteran, kind, but firm — that a boy like Gary — chubby, timid, lazy, vulnerable — needed. And Gary's problems might have remained small if my father had continued to play the role he always had. But everything changed for Gary when Dad died.

Gary. School photo.

CHAPTER 22

Oh, brother

If I was the good boy, my brother Gary was the lost boy.

He was born three years after me and named for my mother's movie heartthrob, Gary Cooper, a tall, sinewy man of few words who epitomized honor, strength and the quiet courage so much admired in those guileless times before the rise of the anti-hero.

My mother's movie hero was a rescuer. But the baby she named after Gary Cooper was not. Instead, he was the one needing rescuing, and she became the rescuer.

Gary neither looked nor acted like anyone's idea of a stoic hero. Except for a short period when he was shooting heroin, Gary was anywhere from pudgy to obese for as long back as I can recall. When we played board games — Monopoly or checkers — and he was about to lose, he'd tip over the board, yell and go red in his big chipmunk cheeks.

Army Mae recalled, "You were a good boy, really. Gary was hard right from the beginning. He was just a difficult kid. Gary was devilish. You could find him down the field there, come home and he'd be covered with dirt. I think he loved rollin' in dirt … You didn't want your hands to get dirty. Gary — wouldn't bother him if he ate it."

Photos taken when he was five and I was eight show me with a normal build, not skinny and certainly not fat, and Gary next to me, his sports coat straining at the buttons, a large, round head, a tender smile on his face that seemed to be saying, "Look, I'm happy. Please be nice to me."

He wasn't a bad kid — maybe a messy kid, a needy kid, but he was never mean or violent or dishonest. That was the case until he became an addict, and then he stole anything he could find in the house that was worth even a few dollars.

How Gary behaved in those first few years, I was too young then to notice or be able to recall these many decades later. But I know how he was by the time he started school, and I wonder if the problems that appeared then went back even further. Was he quick to cry as a baby? Did he demand constant attention? Did he talk late, walk late, have trouble learning his numbers and colors?

Gary was the chubby boy, outwardly cheery with those happy cheeks, but beneath the surface was a sensitivity — perhaps a sadness — expressing a deep need to be taken care of.

In the eighth grade, every student was required to write his autobiography. I found Gary's in my mother's house after she died, 10 loose-leaf lined pages in a stained yellow binder. He was about 13 when he wrote it, yet the handwriting and syntax seem that of a child, not a teenager.

In the first grade, he recalls that his teacher, Sister Hillary, "was very nice" and he did well except for the time he was caught showing another student his good grade on a paper "and sister tore it up for bragging."

On the bottom of the autobiography he had taped his first grade photo. He is wearing a white shirt and a striped bowtie. His head is the shape of a wide "U." His eyebrows are raised and his eyes are looking up, mouth opened, not smiling, all of it leaving the impression of a plea, a plea to take it easy on this fragile soul.

In subsequent years his memories in class essays run mostly along two themes: Was the teacher nice to him, and did he get into trouble? In the second grade he is forced to stand in the back of the room because he and another boy "were always fooling around," but, still, "Sister Monica was very nice."

He recalls a "tragedy" in the fourth grade, the deaths of our father's mother and our mother's brother, Uncle Dean, but he adds that he had fun at Catholic summer camp where there was a dance with the girls from the camp across the lake. He danced with two girls, but didn't like them and left them on the dance floor. Then he danced with a French-Canadian girl "who couldn't speak very good American so I stayed with her."

The fifth grade teacher was "nice" at first, "but then she wasn't." In the sixth grade, Sister Aloysius "was always giving me heck for fooling around." The next year "was just like every other one I had, bad. I progressed and finally I passed to my unbelief." In the eighth grade, he wrote, "I got stuck with a 'crummy' teacher. She's always giving me heck from having my hair in my eyes."

His grades were good at first — all A's and B's in the third grade. The next year, when he is 10 years old, he averaged a C+. The next year, he got D's in four subjects and a C- in effort; the following year, he did just a little better.

With just a couple weeks away from graduating from elementary school and a poor academic record to that point, he declared that he would be going to the Catholic high school, where I was a junior, and then to college.

"In College I hope to major in Math and after graduating get a job in the field of enginerring (sic)."

I don't know how he got this into his head. We didn't know any engineers, but perhaps he made a connection between our father's work with machines and engineering.

Gary had a deep and quiet bond with our father. He sat next to him at dinner and afterwards, when I was out with friends, Gary would stay home. They'd both move to the living room, where Gary would on many nights ask Dad to "tell me about the war."

Dad would go to his bedroom and come back with one of those large cardboard envelopes with a shoestring clasp and take out the items one at a time. The dog tag on a chain: a piece of metal stamped with his name, serial number and the name and address of his mother. Gary would hold it in his hands, put it on, imagining, I suppose, its travel from New Hampshire to California to the Philippines and Japan and back again as it rested on the chest of the gray-haired man right next to him, who was reaching down to the floor for his glass of amber ale.

Neither of us asked why our dad's mother's name and address was on the dog tag, for the thought of our father dead was unfathomable. The bad guys — the Japanese and the Nazis — they died by the scores in the movies we watched. But the good guys got medals and came home to parades.

And Dad had a medal, all right. It was in a blue cardboard box, pinned to matching blue velour backing. The round bronze medal hung from a red and white striped ribbon and was embossed with an eagle, its talons wrapped around a sword. The reverse side states, "For Good Conduct." It was the medal all soldiers got just for serving, unless they were dishonorably discharged. For Gary, though, it was magical, the mark of a true hero, and he could gladly look at it every night.

His favorite movies were "To Hell and Back," the hagiography of WWII Medal of Honor winner Audie Murphy, in which Murphy played himself, and "The Bridge Over the River Kwai," in which Allied prisoners of war prove their mettle against their Japanese captors. His favorite book, dogeared from multiple readings, was "The Rise and Fall of the Third Reich." His father — his own flesh and blood, the man who put his food on the table, drove him to his Little League games, never yelled at him for a bad report card — had been a living player in the greatest drama of the century. How could this tender little boy not attach himself to this anchor.

As I look up from my computer, I see one of Gary's possessions that survived his meager life, one of the few things he bothered to keep safe as he moved from one addiction to another, from home to crash pad, from jail to halfway house and home again. The foot-high piggy bank stands on my bookcase. I call it Sgt. Rock. He is rotund, with bulging cheeks and a sneering lower lip and the stub of a cigar in his left hand — the crusty sergeant you don't cross. A tough guy, a soldier, a man.

Sgt. Rock was a constant reminder my brother kept near him to remind himself of the man he wanted to be.

What Gary and I shared came from those early years on Wentworth Street: the low expectations, the cocoon of the extended family and the unstated place we held as the idealized version of an American child. The difference was that I came through with just enough confidence to step out of the cocoon when the chance came. Gary's chance to go from boy to man, to be more than the needy, overweight kid dubbed "Beachball" by his teammates, never happened. When he was about to be of an age when, despite his reluctance to grow up, he might have become less a boy and more a man, the one person who could have eased that transition disappeared from his life.

And, for the second time in my mother's life, the family burden would fall on her. First, though, my father had to take Gary and me to a baseball game.

My mother, Gary and me in front of our new home on Henry Law Avenue.

CHAPTER 23

The line breaks

Until the spring of 1968, "Boston" had only one meaning for my brother and me. To the country, to the world, Boston was home to some of the greatest universities, the top research hospitals, the harbor where the American Revolution began, world-class museums, libraries and symphonies.

Not to us. All we knew of Boston, all we cared about, was a green-painted jewel box a block off Kenmore Square called Fenway Park.

Once a year, we got to go there with our father. To Gary and me, everything about our annual Sox game was a bigger deal and more exciting than any holiday. We were not a family that travelled. There was no money and little time off for renting a cottage on a lake or a few nights in New York City to see the sights. In all my childhood we took only one trip that required staying in a motel: Gary and I badgered our parents to take us to the Baseball Hall of Fame in Cooperstown, N.Y.

Boston is only 65 miles from Dover, and with the minimal traffic back in the 1950s and 60s, especially on the weekends, it only took a little more than a hour to drive there. But that's not how it felt — it felt like a pilgrimage, a major excursion to not only another state, but to the big, scary city with its tangle of streets and the chance to get lost and end up in the "wrong" neighborhood.

It even intimidated my father, a man who trained on artillery in Texas and then went to war in the Pacific. As soon as I got my driver's license, he had me drive the used Buick into Boston, which I was fine with until we had to go over the Mystic River Bridge with Boston harbor and Charlestown what seemed like a mile below us, and my palms started to sweat and my swallow reflex went haywire.

As the 1967 season began, no one had any expectation the Sox would do any better than they had in the past 20 years — end up at or near the bottom of the American League standings. So when Dad told us he got tickets for the very last game of the season — Oct. 1 — we assumed it would be a game of no consequence. But we didn't really care. All we cared about was going to Fenway and seeing our favorite players, especially the left fielder, Carl Yastrzemski, heir to that baseball god who played that position before Yaz took his place, one Theodore Williams, aka Ted Williams, aka The Kid, aka The Splendid Splinter. In '67, Yaz was the talk of baseball and the hero of all of New England and, in Gary's heart especially, second only to Dad in his pantheon of manhood.

In '67, Yaz led the team to 91 wins and only 70 losses going into that final game. He batted .326 with 44 home runs for the season — the best in the American League, so good he was named Most Valuable Player and won perhaps the rarest of baseball awards — the Triple Crown, given to a player who led the league in batting average, home runs and runs batted in.

Carl Michael Yastrzemski wasn't a quiet, tough New Englander, but he was pretty close — the son of a Long Island potato farmer, Yaz was a man with a firmly set face, who never said a lot and bore the adulation that was showered on him as if he wished home plate would open up and he could disappear with a slight tip of the hat.

I was 19 that year, and Nietzsche, Kerouac, Eldridge Cleaver and Bob Dylan had displaced the ballplayers and boxers I had worshipped just a couple years earlier. But I never considered not going to Fenway — I might have been breaking away from home, but I was unwilling — maybe even constitutionally unable — to challenge my father's expectation of being a good and grateful son.

Less than a year after that game, in the spring of '68, "Boston" would take on another meaning for the Christie family. Not the place you went to sit behind home plate with a hot dog and a Coke, eyes fixed on those brilliant white uniforms glowing against the backdrop of an impossibly green field.

No, "Boston" would have a new, darker meaning for us. But on that early fall day, when the home team players — "The Hawk" Harrelson, Rico Petrocelli, "Gentleman Jim" Lonborg, Elston 'Ellie' Howard, and Yaz, also known as "Captain Carl" — ran out to their positions, Boston was more than ever synonymous with Paradise.

Nineteen sixty-seven, it turned out, was not another "wait 'til next year" season. The team's switch in just one year from bottom of the American League standings to the top was so unexpected it became known as the Impossible Dream. The Boston Red Sox were having one helluva season. With one game to go, they were tied for first place with the Minnesota Twins, and all they had to do to be in first place — which meant winning the American League pennant and going to the World Series — was win this one game.

The game we had tickets for.

Good tickets right behind home plate.

The Red Sox had not won the pennant or played in the World Series in my lifetime, and Dad was just six years old the last time they won the World Series.

So on that October afternoon, when Sox starting pitcher Jim Lonborg went into his windup to throw the first pitch of the game, with dad next to us with his beer and Lucky Strike, Gary and I leaned forward, eyes as open as we could make them, determined to register in our memories every pitch, every hit, every slide, every catch, every throw, every run.

Boston won the game, 5-3, led by Yaz's four hits and two runs batted in. We had been witness to perhaps the most meaningful game in the team's post WWII history, and the player we admired most — whom Gary worshipped until his final breath decades later — had pretty much a perfect day.

(Gary begged me to name our first child Yaz; Yazabelle if it was a girl. We named him Nicholas, but his middle name is Thomas, after Dad.)

The Sox lost the World Series, but for the first time ever, the inevitable, "Wait 'til next year" was not a delusional declaration.

When the next year came, though, when the team returned from Florida spring training, Gary had a fresh interest. Baseball was out. Getting high was in. And Dad was gone.

• • •

"John, John, Gary's run away. I think he's in Boston. You have to go down there and find him. I'm scared to death."

That call from my mother came in the spring of 1968, when I was away at college. It was five months after the death of my father, the man whose quiet authority had until then kept my troubled brother tethered on a thin line to home, to school, to safety.

The line broke just after the Christmas of '67, on a wooden floor stained with machine oil when Thomas Henry Christie, age 58, collapsed and died of a heart attack. This marked the beginning of the end of my mother's good years.

It happened on a Saturday shift he had taken for the overtime pay. In working class homes, the word "overtime" was more than a term for increased pay for increased work — it was like a promotion, like free money, like a gift. It was a magical word. And you took it any time you could because it was the only way to get enough to put aside $20 or $30 towards a used car, a small vacation, a nicer Christmas — or, in my father's case, his son's college tuition and room and board.

A man of his age, a man who worked hard every day and slept poorly every night due to a hyperactive thyroid, should have been able to take off a Saturday in the middle of the holidays. But with my college tuition to pay for, on top of the usual expenses and perhaps some extras for the holidays, he needed money. So he put in the overtime.

Not that I appreciated his sacrifice then, as I do now, even though it probably cost him his health and maybe his life. No, I mourned him only briefly at the time, and between his death and that call from my mother, if anything I kept myself at an even greater distance from home than before.

After the Christmas break and the funeral that interrupted it, I returned to my college dorm and the life I lived there as though nothing had happened. All I thought about was new pals on the dorm floor; parties and beer drinking; Saturday night dates; the college newspaper; pickup games of basketball and touch football; lectures by inspiring writers and thinkers — and a part-time job to pay for tuna sandwiches at the student union and beer on the weekends.

My father had just died; my mother was a sudden widow, still working her job at the GE factory; and my younger brother was bereft and adrift. Instead of going home now and then — home was only five miles from the campus — I was staying up late reading "On the Road" or hanging out at bars that didn't take a good look at my phony ID.

I heard so much in that phone call from my mother. Not just the terror and panic in her words, but anger. Anger not just at Gary, but at me, too: Why wasn't I saving her from this fear. Why was I away at college, living on my own, escaping from her and from the messes Gary was creating.

But back then, I was a callow college boy, I didn't know much about her past or, if I even had, I might have put it out of mind. Instead, I was stuck with how to reply to what I felt at the time was her ridiculous and naïve idea that I could find one 17-year-old in a city of a half a million people. I knew I could not tell her that unless I wanted to hear the panic and anger explode with multiple goddamns and Jesus-Mary-and-Josephs, at me, at Gary, at Gary's new druggie friends, at her family for not doing enough to help her. (Later, when Gary ran away even further, to California, she called her baby sister who lived in the San Fernando Valley to instruct her to find Gary, and she got angry when my aunt told her how big the state was.)

My mother knew Boston was bigger than Dover and California bigger yet, but those facts were not what mattered to her. What mattered was that she had a crisis — and that turned out to be no exaggeration. What back then I dismissed as an irrational and panicky idea — that Gary could be found and brought home — I now see was my way of avoiding too much responsibility. Maybe it was an improbable quest, but she wasn't making it because she wasn't as smart as her Joe College son or too upset to think clearly. She had just lost her husband, she had lost her father when she was but a child and now she was losing one of two sons. She wasn't acting out of anything but a mother's unbreakable bond to her children.

I'm sure she was as mystified as I was and still am about what there was in Gary that made him so different from me, given how determined my parents were to treat us equally, how we came from the same gene pool, how there was no obvious medical reason we knew of then or now to explain Gary's problems. Where did his failure to grow up, or even want to grow up, come from? Why wasn't he willing — even eager like every other boy — to put the low-demands of childhood behind in return for the pride that comes from seeing yourself as a man, not boy.

I'm no shrink and my attempts to get one of Gary's psychiatrists — one of his many therapists — to show me his records was met with a firm "no." But I know a little about human behavior and one of the basic needs we all have is a need to belong. Mack's gang provided me with that, but Gary was too young to be part of the group, and, selfishly, I would have vetoed him if he tried. That was my world, and I didn't need a little brother whose nickname was Beachball showing up and either embarrassing me or needing rescuing during our trouble-making.

Every summer until he was about 12, he played youth league baseball, where he either struck out or, employing his considerable heft, hit it over the outfielders' heads, but he'd only get to first base because he was too over-weight to get safely to second. This was well before the time when anyone felt even a bit of guilt for shunning someone because of their weight. No one had any compunction about calling such kids "fatso." Some other overweight boy who had a bit of cockiness in him might have fought back with his own name–calling ("four-eyes" was good for kids who wore glasses or the much crueler "retard" for someone not too smart), but Gary, like me, was not raised to be mean to anyone, even if they deserved it. And he was so vulnerable, he was probably afraid that if he escalated the name-calling, it might get worse than "Hey, Beachball" back at him.

The world outside of home and family was often just too much for Gary. Even home was sometime too much for him to take in his stride. When we were both young, perhaps when he was five or six and I was eight or nine, we played together more out of convenience than any special closeness.

Between our three-year age difference and our different personalities, I didn't want to be around him much. He was my brother, and I did play games and toss around the baseball with him, went places with him and my parents, but we were never great pals, never best friends. I had unstuck myself — or at least was trying to — from the expectations of home, while Gary seemed to want to stay in that bubble no matter his age.

By the time Dad had died we were even less close. I was a "college man," and Gary was a near recluse who was barely making it through high school. I had plenty of pals, girlfriends and summer and after-school jobs that gave me enough spending money for Saturday night movies, gas for my car, week-ly haircuts and getting my button-down shirts pressed so I could look sharp for those dates. My identity had gone from the good boy of Wentworth Street to one of Mack's gang and, now, I saw myself as a pretty cool fellow, Mr. Independent in a navy V-neck sweater and loafers with no socks, on my way to being a writer.

In my self-absorption, I had, without making a conscious decision, put more than three years between my brother and me. I had, with no regrets, thoughtlessly put him in my rear view mirror.

All of Gary's sense of "belonging" had been supplied by Dad — until Dad was gone. If that loss had happened in another era — say the Fifties — Gary might have found another safe world where he could belong. But Gary's sudden need for a new place to belong, a substitute for what he got at home from his father, came at the worse possible time for someone like him.

The year Dad died was 1968, the year that The Sixties — not the numeral decade but the idea of The Sixties — reached its apex, or perhaps its nadir. The Summer of Love was a year old, and the counterculture — and also the mainstream culture it rebelled against — were both starting to be painted black. Two assassinations took away leaders — call them father figures: Martin Luther King and Robert F. Kennedy. The Tet offensive made it clear even to Walter Cronkite, another father-like figure that Gary would watch sitting next to his actual father, that the tens of thousands of boys my age and nearly my brother's were dying in Vietnam for no good reason. And the hippie culture, once all flowers behind the ear and jangling guitars, was morphing into a druggie culture, a place where all you had to do to belong was grow your hair long and use what money you had to get yourself and your "friends" high.

Perfect timing for a lost boy, and all he had to do to belong was get himself to Boston, where clots of bandana-wearing kids like him congregated in the darker corners of the Boston Common.

I estimate Gary showed up there around May 1, 1968. It was likely the only time he had been in Boston for any other reason than to see a Red Sox game.

Only seven months before Gary ran away to the seedier parts of Boston, he and my father and I had been sitting a few rows behind home plate at Fenway, transfixed by Lonborg's pitch and every play that followed.

Gary, probably taken in his 30s
when he was living at home.

CHAPTER 24

Dover to Boston to The Haight

"Okay, okay, Ma. I'll come by tomorrow and get your car and go to Boston and look for him."

"But where's he going to sleep tonight? He took ten dollars from my pocketbook, but that's not enough. Ohhhh, John, John, I don't know what I'm going to do with that kid."

When I went home the next day my mother sat at the kitchen table, ashtray in front of her, already full with bent butts. By now, my mother's figure had gone from the fashionable girl in the picture in front of city hall to a shape that required she wear large, loose and flowing dresses, a face becoming fuller and puffier with the years, her voice so hoarse from cigarettes that on the phone she was often mistaken for a man.

There was no order to what she told me, just a random series of Gary's screw-ups, delivered sometimes with clenched fists, sometimes in profane hysteria — "That little shit!" — and at times with resignation, all of it a foretelling of the emotions she would endure from that time, when Gary was just

16 years old, until his last day on this earth.

He had been skipping school regularly, but she didn't know that at first because Gary had been forging her name on excuse letters to the principal's office. Gary was already a mediocre student and after my father's death, he didn't even try to do his homework or pass a test, so it didn't take the suspicious nuns at St. Thomas long to figure out Gary was not home sick with the flu, and the principal called my mother to check on those letters.

My mother understood why Gary didn't want to go to school. During Dad's wake at the McCooey Funeral Home, Gary had sat in the last row of the folding chairs, his frame straining at the buttons of his dress shirt, his tie loose and crooked, his elbows on his knees, his head cupped in his hands. At the front of the parlor, Dad's body lay in its walnut casket. He had been dressed in his go-to-church brown suit, a white shirt and, as recognition of his love for his boys, my mother had chosen as his tie one Gary and I had given him for Christmas when we much younger, a silk tie with the head of a regal horse embroidered in the center. We thought this was the height of fashion. It isn't now and it wasn't then and Dad, who earlier photos showed was a dapper dresser, donned the garish tie many a Sunday just to please us.

The etiquette at Catholic wakes requires mourners to get in line to take a few moments at the open casket and kneel down, your face just a foot or so from the face of the deceased, say a silent prayer and move on. I was grateful for the tradition that others probably see as ghoulish — there is no denying the finality of the loss, no compartmentalizing of your feelings to escape your deepest feeling you are literally staring death in the face. Until that moment, for me, the words "My father is dead" were just words. When I saw his face, once so florid, now drained of color, and that tie, the grief that had eluded me until then rushed into my chest like I was drowning in seawater.

Gary, though, would not get anywhere near the casket. My mother asked him, Nana and Army Mae offered to go with him, but he would not budge. They didn't press him, though. My family all knew about Gary's attachment to Dad and felt nothing but sadness for what was obvious: For Gary, Dad's death was unfathomable, unbearable — and it was undoing him before our very eyes.

One of the nuns who taught Gary at St. Thomas was there representing the school. She went up to Gary and told him he had to go pray at the casket, it was his duty as a son and good Catholic, that "God required it."

Gary just sat there and didn't move.

She gave up then, but the next time Gary went to school — probably a couple of days after the wake — she made him stand up in class while she told the other students that Gary was a "baby" because he refused to show his father respect at the wake.

My mother — not a Catholic — called the principal and told her off, probably, given her anger, in not very nice terms.

"I got Sister Dorothea on the phone and told her that I had been baking for every bakery sale at St. Joseph's and St. Mary's and St. Thomas. And I go to work every day to pay those tuitions. And I made sure you boys never missed Mass, and this is what I get! She didn't even apologize."

Sitting at that kitchen table, she said she couldn't blame Gary for not wanting to go to St. Thomas any more.

But he could have told her that he wanted to change schools, could have easily transferred to the public high school, but there was more going on than his humiliation by the nun.

Where was he when he was supposed to be doing his sophomore year? Gary wasn't much of a sneak. He was no more interested in covering his tracks than doing his homework, and my mother decided to do a little investigating. First thing a worried mother does: checks the kid's bedroom closet and dresser. In the top drawer, barely hidden under a pair of socks, was a roach — the remains of a marijuana joint.

I'm sure my mother had never seen marijuana before, but she read the newspapers and news magazines and figured out pretty quickly that Gary was "doing drugs."

Gary might not have been a good liar, but he was quick at it and gave her the usual excuse — it belonged to a friend.

"'Who are these friends?' I asked him. He wouldn't tell me so I went and found out myself."

After he left the house one day, she waited a bit and then drove around Dover's downtown looking for him. She saw him coming out of an apartment house off the city's upper square. When Gary came home, she asked who lived there and what they were doing. Gary slammed his fist on the kitchen table and walked away.

Gary wanted out. Out of school, where he didn't do well, where the nuns scared him and where he had few if any friends. He wanted out of home, where my mother expected not much of him — go to school, do his homework, pick up after himself, have some sort of interests besides TV — but it was more than he wanted to even try to deliver. He wanted out of a world that, I found out later from looking at the few letters he wrote, made him —

in his words — "nervous."

"Nervous" was my family's name for what others called anxiety. My mother often said she was having a "nervous breakdown," but I found out years later that almost everyone in her family had been diagnosed with anxiety. And Gary had it bad. When Dad died, I suspect Gary's anxiety peaked and without a father's approbation, there was no one to stop him from seeking a refuge from all that plagued him — his failures, his grief, his anxiety, his isolation.

Neither my mother nor I know exactly how Gary came to get his first joint, but we found out later that he had met a girl named Diane, whose name he had tattooed on his arm, at that seedy apartment. From what I could gather from my mother, she used Gary to get drugs, first marijuana and, later, heroin.

"She wasn't really his girlfriend, but she made him think she was," my mother told me.

On a dreary day in May, I parked my mother's car in the underground lot beneath Boston Common and walked the perimeter and the pathways of the 50-acre park at the foot of Beacon Hill, a place where 20 years later I would come to work as a reporter covering the statehouse on the top of the hill.

Gary would not have been hard to spot. He was about average height for a 16-year-old, but overweight. He left home wearing a blue windbreaker that I would recognize quickly if I ran across him. His hair was still short, which also would have made him stand out among the hippies I saw walking in the Common, gathering on benches or wandering nearby in the Combat Zone, home to strip clubs, street walkers and drug dealers.

I walked that end of the city a couple times, then widened my search to the back side of the Hill, where there were a lot of student apartments, then moved closer to Park Plaza, where kids like Gary would be attracted to the head shops and music stores.

I took the T — Boston's subway system — up to Kenmore Square and walked around Fenway Park. The Sox were playing on the road that day, but, still, Gary might wander around the outside of the park hoping it would make him feel closer to Dad.

I drove back to my mother's house. She was waiting in the breezeway, probably for hours, keeping an eye out for me so she could know even before I got to the end of the driveway if Gary was in the car with me.

She peppered me with questions, coming so fast there was no time to answer between questions. "Where did you look? Did you look where all the other kids hang out? Did you ask people if they had seen him? Did you talk to the police?"

Ask the notoriously cynical Boston cops about one runaway kid who'd only been away a couple days? No. And the hippies I talked to and showed Gary's picture to just shrugged and asked me for a dollar.

It was futile, as I knew it was likely to be. But it wasn't just my mother's fear that sent me on my quixotic attempt. I would have loved to have found Gary and maybe talk him into coming home and perhaps if I had, his future — and my mother's — might have been different, although it is hard to think that he wouldn't have run away again.

I like to think now that for the hours I was searching in vain, those were hours when my mother had some hope that Gary was not lost to her.

All we could do now was wait.

About a week later my mother got a collect call from Gary. Somehow — I never found out the details — he had got himself to the mecca of drugs and crash pads: He was in Haight-Ashbury in San Francisco. He didn't tell her much. He claimed to be OK and ended the call before she could get much out of him, but at least she knew he was alive and she was grateful he had thought at least that much about her fears.

The kid had hardly ever been away from home before and within a couple weeks he was all the way across the country and had become one of the thousands, tens of thousands, of dropouts looking for something they didn't have in their lives. Plenty of creativity came out of The Haight district — music, art, theater, fashion — but for kids like Gary all that freedom — free love, free to get high, free to beg on the streets for spare change — came to them when they were too young, too immature, too much in need of belonging.

It was not like the Janis Joplin song — "Freedom's just another word for nothing left to lose." Freedom for Gary and too many like him was another word for giving up and giving in. Fuck yourself up, fast as possible. Anything for a few minutes or maybe an hour of dreamy relief from whatever they were trying to escape.

Weeks went by without another word until my mother got a call from the sheriff in Cheyenne, Wyoming. Another panicky call to me to come home so she tell could me in person what the sheriff told her:

"He told me that Gary was in the hospital with an infection in his arm from a bad needle and that if I don't send him a plane ticket out of Wyoming he's going to put Gary in jail."

For now, the anger was fully gone, replaced by resignation, fear and despair. A year ago her youngest son was a homebody, a kid from an upstanding family that never had a smudge on its reputation. Not even a parking ticket.

How had he gone so fast from being a 16-year-old boy in a small New Hampshire mill town who collected baseball cards, to a heroin addict? This was not 2018, when rural states like New Hampshire were plagued with opioid and fentanyl deaths. This was 50 years before that, when you had to know someone who knew someone even to get an ounce of marijuana. Gary had moved fast from over-indulging in my mother's weekly trip to Harvey's Bakery for cream-filled maple squares to Boston for marijuana to San Francisco for heroin.

Gary had no money and, we found out when he got home, had been hitchhiking back east when he got sick. The boy we saw when he got back was not the one who had run away. The rolls of belly fat were nearly gone, his brown hair ran over his eyes and down his back in matted clumps, but it was his eyes that told the story best.

Once, they had been watery, pleading eyes that turned to childlike wonder when he talked baseball or Mom arrived home with a treat. Now, his brown eyes were black dots, drained of life, eyes that I realize now told my mother and me all we ever needed to know about the years to come. Gary had left home on a mission to destroy himself as fast as he could and now he was sitting at that kitchen table, in his usual seat next to Dad's now-vacant place, and laying his right arm on the table so my mother could remove the eight inches of gauze between his wrist and elbow.

Beneath the bandage lay an excavation of flesh.

Glistening with ooze and tinted an angry pink, the trench of infected tissue the ER doctor had scraped from around Gary's wrist was the shape of a jagged heart. It must have been almost two inches wide and three or more inches long.

"Jesus, Mary and Joseph, Gary, what did you do to yourself," my mother said as she removed the last layer of wet gauze.

It was not a question, and Gary gave no reply.

The infection got better, but the risk of another — or worse — didn't stop Gary.

My mother and my son, Nick, Christmas at my home in Maine in 2000.

CHAPTER 25

One blissful moment

Now, Gary was living at home on Henry Law Avenue, except when he'd be away at some crash pad and wouldn't come home until he needed something — a decent meal, an escape from his druggie friends. Then he'd return to his mother, who took him in because she loved him, because she wanted to protect him and because she believed if he was home maybe she could save him. But, I think more than any other reason, she took him in, never threw him out was because if he was home, those were days or even just hours where she would not have to live in dread of another one of those late-night calls.

Some came from the cops — "Is Gary S. Christie your son?" "Yes." "We have him at the station for possession of a controlled substance." Or "We just transported him to the hospital with a possible overdose."

Or maybe the call was from Gary or one his pals. "Ma, I'm OK. I just need a ride home." "Where are you?" "Lawrence. In Massachusetts." (Back then and still now, that huge mill town just north of Boston was a central

139

distribution point in northern New England for drugs from New York City.)

She would drive to Lawrence, to some street corner where she might well have been robbed. Gary would get in the car, she would scream at him and then he'd sleep — pass out — all the way home.

In time, I knew and all of my mother's sisters and brothers knew and all of her friends knew: "Do Not Call" after the sun went down. Nighttime and a ringing phone meant just one thing to her: one of these days it would be, "Your son is dead."

On the rare times when I had to call her at night, before I could get in a word that everything was fine, she'd say, with a rapid jumpiness, 'What! What! What's wrong!"

When Gary's addiction was at its peak, he would — like any addict — do whatever he had to do to get the money for heroin. My Boy Scout knapsack, my early rock 'n' roll albums, my baseball glove, all sold for probably very little, and that's nothing compared to what he took from my mother: money from her wallet, her prescriptions he could sell on the street (did he ever consider that she needed these to stay alive?) and even her wedding ring, which he stole, sold and never could remember who he sold it to so she could buy it back. He was so far on the other side of decency that I believe it never occurred to him that that ring was not just his mother's possession — a woman he resented as much as he needed — but it had begun its life in the hands of his revered father.

With the addictions, and whatever caused them to begin with, came hallucinations, paranoia and unpredictable outbursts of anger. All of it another cross for my mother to bear.

In the darkness of his bedroom, the room that once had been a small but cozy den, my mother would hear him screaming like a little boy who had seen the devil. She'd run to his room, and he'd be grabbing at his crotch, yelling, "Stop! Stop! Stop! It's going away, it's going away."

He thought his genitals were receding.

He knew it wasn't really happening, but he said he was having the recurring hallucination from one of 60 LSD trips he had taken in his teens and twenties.

When he finally got off the drugs and the beer — sometime in his late forties, still living with my mother — he moved his addiction to food. He'd sleep until the afternoon, get up and eat multiple meals of rice pilaf, potatoes, hamburgers — whatever my mother was willing to make — and wash it all down with glass after glass of milk. A diet designed to make you feel continuously full, to abuse a legal substance to recreate the relief that drugs and beer had once given him.

I can credit him with one thing he did that made my mother's life less stressful. By transferring his addiction to food, he found a means to fill up the hole in his life in a way that doesn't get you in trouble with the police, doesn't have you on the streets buying drugs, doesn't have you driving back from a bar drunk. And that took the anxiety about late-night calls out of the equation.

Have I been too hard on my brother? As I was bringing up my memories of his life and his life with my mother, experts were debating the issue of whether drug addicts bear any responsibility for their actions. Some said they don't, that the need, the craving was not a choice.

"Drug addiction, we now know, is a chronic brain disease whose hallmark feature is an inability to exert control over the impulse to use drugs despite negative consequences," a doctor told the *Boston Globe* in 2017.

But in the same article, a psychiatrist said the threat of going to jail or other "sanctions" — perhaps being told to leave your parent's home unless you clean up—"gives the addict an extremely powerful incentive to stay clean."

No one made Gary put that first needle in his arm. When he was in jail for stealing a TV to sell for drug money or in rehab, he'd get off drugs but then start up again when he was released. Was the siren call of heroin so enticing that the decision was out of his control? Didn't he remember what it had done to him and to his mother? Did he just want so badly to get on that slow train to oblivion — and death — that any attempt at reasoning with himself lasted about a second.

The most charitable explanation for my brother's drug use is it began because he was feeling lost and depressed after our father died and the drug is so powerful — and Gary's need so great — that it was nearly impossible to kick the habit. Friends who know the story of my brother wonder why I don't necessarily see it that way, but none of them, as far as I know, had a family member who was a drug addict. But when I talk to brothers, sisters, daughters, sons, husbands or wives who experienced what I did and what my mother, especially, did, they get it: It's easy to cast a sympathetic eye on the addict or alcoholic when it's not your life that's being ruined.

Even if I excuse Gary for what he did to himself because, as the experts say, it's a disease, what excuse is there for dragging another human being — the one who gave you life and cleaned your wounds and made a home for you — to that same hell.

Even after Gary was off drugs and beer, life with him was still hard for our mother — the bad temper, the constant shopping and cooking and cleaning up for him, the lack of any help in caring for their home, all of it meant she never had her own life. Gary would even complain of being left alone when she went to lunch with her friends.

"I'd come home, and he'd be an in ugly mood," she told me. "Ugly" was one of my mother's go-to words. If you were in an ugly mood you were just this side of tossing plates or kicking the dog or tipping over the kitchen table.

It wasn't all ugly as Gary grew older. He might not do anything around the house to help out, but he'd drive Mom to the doctor or, on a nice day, take her to the beach, a small favor but one she was so grateful for that she'd boast about it on the phone to me.

And Gary was gentle and loving to my son, who remembers Gary more as an oversized kid than an adult uncle. They'd read comic books together or play board games, and when Nick was around 12, Gary would take him to shoot pool and then get an ice cream. I have a photo of the two of them in our pool in Florida, with seven-year-old Nick riding atop his uncle's shoulders as Gary wades into the pool like a giant servant attending to his royal charge.

By the time Gary was a middle-aged man — his hair half gray, his beseeching eyes behind thick glasses, his condition so poor he was out of breath just getting up from his easy chair — my mother was in her late 70s. She had emphysema and lung cancer from a lifetime of smoking cigarettes and breathing in solder fumes from her job at GE.

As she neared her final days, did she look back at her life in Dover and do the math I have done? Add up the good years and the bad ones and see how few landed on the good side: perhaps 20 or 25 years of her 79. Is that what she was thinking about when she sat in the breezeway in one of her big loose dresses, sat there with her cup of coffee, craving the cigarettes she had given up after turning purple at the hairdresser and being rushed to the emergency room? I hope not. I hope she had found some happier times to recall, but I can see her now as I open the door to the breezeway and, unless I had her grandson with me, that mouth was taut and her eyes seemed to be looking back to every hurt, every betrayal, everyone else's failure to help her. An ugly mood, I thought.

That mood may have its roots all the way back to Nana's village in Turkey. The study by the Boston University researcher of the effects of the Armenian Genocide on the children and grandchildren of victims said:

"Some have said that because of this past and the sufferings of their parents, they were required to be serious and in some sense, almost sad."

My mother's mother arrived in the U.S. full of sadness — "It's a sad life," she told Tammy, thinking about her murdered father, her mother dying on a forced march, her brother starving to death. On Wentworth Street, Nana lost her husband and, my mother — only 10 — lost her father: more sadness, a sadness that for my mother deepened into bitterness because of her demanding childhood and her desperate son.

Maybe that was what I saw on her face.

When, after Dad's death, the bad years came back, they were worse than ever. Gary walked into the deep end and from that day until his final day, I recall only a few times when I saw my mother relaxed and maybe even happy.

She came to my house in Maine for Christmas in 2000. Nick was home from college, and I took a photo of the two of them on our sofa. Nick is smiling broadly, almost laughing, sitting a few feet away from his grandmother. They have just exchanged a comment or a story, I don't recall, but whatever it was, it put a look on her face I never saw in any of the many photos of her. Maybe it was just being in the presence of her healthy grandson who loved to be around her as much as she loved having him near.

She is nicely dressed in navy with a bright red scarf. A quiet smile below closed eyes, like she is contemplating a moment, a feeling she wants to hold in her memory forever. My mother's blissful look says she knows that Nick knows she loves him. I cannot look at that photo and not weep, weep for the happiness in it and weep for the happiness — or maybe just the absence of unhappiness — that she was missing for so many years.

My mother, "Kay" Christie, on the job making electric meters
at the GE plant in Somersworth, N.H.

CHAPTER 26

Freedom came too late

My mother's final years with Gary were, at least, free of drugs and drinking, but he was dependent on her like a child. He was depressed or worse, in despair, for he was in his fifties and had wasted his life and nothing promising lay ahead. When that got the best of him, when he was in one of those ugly moods, he had only one place to put his anger — at my mother. He'd yell, punch the walls, blame her for his life, get so angry that she'd worry he'd hit her. He never did, but when she told me about his outbursts I felt I had no choice but to confront him on one of my visits.

We got in my car and drove to a local pool hall — Gary was a pretty good pool player — and on the ride back I told him that if he ever even touched our mother, I'd break his neck. Probably not the most effective way to get his attention, but my anger and fear were stronger than my good sense.

"Okay, John," was all he said and was quiet the rest of way home.

Later, my mother told me that I hurt his feelings so much that she'd rather I not ever remonstrate with him again. She was still protecting him and sacrificing not just her happiness, but perhaps her safety.

The following April, one day after Gary's 51st birthday, I was driving home from work in the late afternoon when I got a call on my cell phone.

"John, your brother is dead."

My mother went on to tell me what happened, but all I could keep saying to myself was, "My brother is dead. MY brother, MY brother." I kept repeating those words because, I think now, I believed I was supposed to save Gary. He was mine, like my house was mine, my son was mine — as if it was my responsibility to see that nothing bad happened to something that was "mine."

When I was a boy, Gary was the little brother who I played with because he was there. When I was a teenager and in college and then a young man, I tried — and mostly succeeded — in making sure he was not a drag on the life I wanted.

When I was older and had my own family, and he was devastating my mother's life, I still kept some distance, but treated him more kindly, visiting him in jail (he stole a TV to sell to buy drugs), the state mental hospital, where he was sent rather than jail, and treatment centers that rarely had much effect.

I invited him and my mother to stay with us in Florida; I came back to Dover for many holidays. I was around some of the time and now and then would talk to him about his problems, but it never went far enough to truly confront what was happening. Neither of us wanted that kind of deeply honest, blunt relationship.

I didn't want it because I didn't know what to do. Should I be sympathetic and understanding, which felt hypocritical, because I was as mad as I was sad about how he lived? When I tried that approach, he didn't seem to want to talk about what he was doing or how he felt because he was embarrassed in front of his big brother to be such a screw-up. Or I could play the authority figure and berate him, threaten, grab him by the shoulders and tell him to grow the fuck up. I tried that to no success.

I was angry, but not without any sympathy, and, besides, my mother got angry at him, and it did no good. I'd have my go at him and then go home to wherever I was living at the time — Massachusetts, Florida, Maine — and my mother would have to deal with the aftermath.

Gary's habit was to stay up all night, often falling asleep eventually in his oversized recliner. On the morning of April 15, 2002, my mother got up as usual and Gary was still in the recliner, but he couldn't be wakened and was cold to the touch.

The death certificate states the cause of death was "arteriosclerotic cardio-vascular disease"— a bad heart. They were the same words as on our father's death certificate from 35 years earlier. On Gary's paperwork under "Other significant conditions" there was one word: "Obesity."

He had eaten himself to an early grave. It took him 35 years of filling his body up with heroin, LSD, beer, pizza, hamburgers, potatoes, rice, Pepsi, milk, etc., to make himself feel good for a moment while simultaneously eventually getting where he wanted to be: Not in this world, where he never found a place for himself.

Now, when I bring Gary up from my memory bank, I am no longer angry. Now, I feel confused, remorseful and wistful.

I still don't know and will never know with certainty why he turned out the way he did. I like to believe that if my father had lived another 10 years, he would have eased Gary into adulthood. My mother told me that Dad always hoped that at least one of his sons would live at home as an adult, which was why he had plans to add a bathroom on the second floor where Gary and I shared a bedroom. That would have been perfect for Gary.

But there was no father to shepherd the lost boy, and I — the big brother — did not take on the father role. I was off to build a career and have a family. I had neither the interest, the opportunity nor, perhaps, a deep enough love to be the father Gary needed.

I made some attempts, though, from threats to entreaties to one-time gestures, like taking him to see Yastrzemski's last game as a Red Sox in 1983, when Gary was 32 and I was 35. It was a perfect day, even if Gary did drink too much beer, because it was the Christie boys again, sitting behind home plate again like we did with Dad, with our hero playing left field again. When the game ended, Yaz ran the perimeter of the field, tipping his hat to the fans, all cheering wildly, many with tears in their eyes. As Yaz passed where we sat, Gary turned to me and said, "Thank you, John."

I'd hoped that gratitude and that feeling of returning to the days before Dad died and Gary went off the deep end, might inspire him to change, to honor his father by being a better son. But I gave one day too much credit. The continuous beer drinking should have been a clue — Gary was back to drugs within days after the game.

Maybe there was little I could do to get Gary to change. To get off drugs or beer or gluttony, to get him to find a job, to get him to stop being a worry and a burden to our mother. Maybe he was lost the day Dad died because everything that was done for him after that — my mother's devotion, the

stints at rehab, the sessions with psychologists and addiction counselors —
failed to make a difference.

After Gary died, I found a typed three-page poem he had written stashed
in a dresser drawer. In it, he imagines "something moving in the back of my
brain." Is it, he writes, something that will "make me sing, fill the air with a
raspy tune."

It turns out, that what was moving in the back of his brain was not what
he wished for. Instead, the mysterious "it" grows bigger and bigger

until it breaks my head in half
leaving nothing but
a smoking shotgun.

It was my mother who had to live with the man-boy whose frightful
thoughts could only stop if he lulled himself into oblivion.

She had six months of freedom from Gary, from the time he died of a
heart attack until the time she died of lung cancer. If she had been healthy,
she might have been able to mourn Gary but live her remaining days guilt-
free because she knew he would have died years, maybe decades, earlier except for her devotion. Free of Gary's moods, free of her fears he would explode, free of her suspicions he might return to drugs or alcohol, she could
have lived the same life as her friends who had retired — lunches out, trips
to music theatres, bus excursions to the casinos in Connecticut, doting on
her grandson.

But, instead, all her time from Gary's death to her own was spent getting
chemotherapy for her lung cancer or recovering from the treatment. I took
her to many of those appointments, driving down the two hours from Maine
to Dover as often as she needed. I offered to take her out for meals, do her
shopping, clean up around the house, whatever would make her life easier.
But she kept saying she was too tired to go to restaurants, she had everything
she needed, "Just bring me to the doctor's when you can."

On Oct. 8, 2002, I arrived at 167 Henry Law Ave. to take her to an appointment with her oncologist. Neither she nor I were expecting anything but
discouraging news because at the previous appointment the doctor had said
the chemo wasn't doing much good anymore. "But come in a couple weeks
and we'll see what else we can do," he said, patting my mother on the arm.

I went through the breezeway, her favorite place to sit and smoke and
read her magazines when she still smoked, and tried the door to the kitchen,
where normally she would be waiting, dressed in her coat, pocketbook on her
lap, anxious to be on time for her appointment.

The door was locked. She wasn't sitting in the kitchen. I knocked and yelled. No response.

I tried to keep my dread down, tried to keep breathing and act quickly to find the key under the doormat, unlock the door and rush to her bedroom.

The oxygen mask she wore to bed was on the floor. Her head tilted off the edge of the pillow and her face was immobile, her mouth parted, her eyes open but snuffed out.

I shook her, put my face to her mouth to feel for a breath, put my hands on her cheeks — no reaction, not a hint of breathing, no warmth.

At her funeral, I thanked her family and friends for caring for her in her last days: "When the demands increased, you came through like saints."

"My mother," I said, "was a sort of saint in her own right. Who among us can say he saved a life. My mother did. She saved my brother's life many times. From the age of 16, when my father died, Gary led a troubled life. For the next 35 years, my mother rescued him over and over again from his addictions, his despair and his depressions. That stubborn streak of hers refused to give up on Gary. Her love was not limited to the good times."

UNH Professor of English Donald M. Murray.
Photo courtesy Milne Special Collections and Archives Department,
University of New Hampshire Library, Durham, N.H.

CHAPTER 27

The Professor calls home

My journey to self-understanding required me to make a trip to the end
of my adolescence and my college days. It required another deep dive into
my memories and my emotions, back to the day I lost a father and gained
one, and I unknowingly started on a fresh path that would help redeem the
sufferings of my family.

The redemption had begun with being the boy who did not have to suffer
as they had and one day, perhaps, could work with his mind, not his hands.

The rebellion Mack and the gang set in motion looks like a rejection of
what my family wanted from me. But it was a rebellion tempered by a loyalty to Nana and the uncles and aunts and to my quiet and dignified father
and to my mother, with her broken body, solder-scorched fingers and bitter
memories.

All of these feelings — the weight of my family's past, the nascent independent streak, the aspiration to join the middle class — came with me to
college, waiting for a resolution.

The University of New Hampshire is only a few miles from Dover and to save money I lived at home my freshman year, commuting by car to the campus. It wasn't the same as "going to college." It was more like still being in high school but taking harder courses. So, even though it was another expense for my parents, I started my second year in a dorm on the campus.

I may have been a "college man," but I was still a working-class boy with fantasies of what college meant and what it would lead to. I had seen nearly every adult I knew leave home every day in a rough cotton uniform or drab work clothes, show up for work at a big, loud plant humming with machinery, and come home exhausted, dirty and sweaty. I had done those same jobs and worse myself: garbage man, grave digger, janitor, road worker, grocery boy. I had worked on a factory line pouring liquid foam into hot molds to make car seats. I had pushed carts overflowing with leather scraps around shoe shops. I had unloaded bags of feed from claustrophobic freight cars in the middle of a heat wave. And even while I was taking a full course load at college I was emptying the trash, vacuuming the rugs, and waxing the floors of my local high school two nights a week.

I wanted no more of that. I wanted someday to put on a fresh shirt and suit every morning and drive my Jaguar (white, with leather seats) to my law office. I had little idea what a lawyer did. But I knew what he didn't have to do — which was all the stuff I'd grown up doing. That was all that mattered to me.

So I declared myself pre-law and majored in political science. But — again, with fantasies about the middle class filling my head — I decided that one skill a lawyer needs is to be a good writer, because in the movies and TV shows I watched lawyers were always having to write briefs. (I was disabused of the idea that these had to be well written once I became a reporter and actually read a lot of briefs, which were models of turgid prose and obfuscation.) I didn't see any brief-writing courses in the UNH catalogue. What I saw were courses in writing fiction (which I rarely read), poetry (which I knew was over my head) and news (but I was going to be a lawyer, not a reporter).

However there was a course called "Expository Writing." I didn't know what that was, but it wasn't any of the kinds of writing I didn't want, so by process of elimination, I signed up for it.

The class was held on the main floor of one of the oldest buildings on campus, Hamilton Smith Hall, a classic brick-and-ivy edifice. Its hardwood floors were worn down by thousands of students over many decades stomping around in shoes wet from the New Hampshire winters and crusted with the salt and gravel the school's work crews spread on the slippery walkways. Bearded philosophy professors moved through the hallways, smoking their pipes; history teachers with flowing gray hair were trailed by young women in plaid skirts; the odd woman prof, aloof and hollow-cheeked, wearing a two-piece suit and heels, raised a cigarette to her lipsticked-lips, the very image of a 1960s intellectual.

This was college as I imagined it: A place to think, not work; a place to read and philosophize, not produce. Then I went into Room 220, where Professor of English Donald M. Murray was teaching expository writing. What was this? Instead of a normal classroom, with seats and desks in rows facing the front of the room, where the teacher stood at a lectern, there were long tables arranged in a rectangle with typewriters at every chair. To me, who had never seen a newsroom, it looked like a typing pool for secretaries. I didn't know how to type and had no interest in learning to or in taking a course with any kind of machine in the room.

But, I still had plenty of the good boy in me. I had signed up for this, so I obediently took a seat. Soon a side door that led to a private office opened up and in walked a bear. A bear of a man. Six-feet, wavy gray hair, salt-and-pepper beard, a broad chest and a broad belly. No pipe, no tweed jacket, no tie. Instead, khaki pants, a plain shirt and a colorful set of suspenders. And the guy was smiling, a disarming grin under that mostly white mustache. Was he happy to see us, a bunch of underclassman who very likely did not know how to write (me) or were afraid of writing (me) or (the worst ones) already thought they could write because they got A's in high school composition (not me)?

As time went on, I came to realize I had accidentally signed up with one of the top teachers on the campus. He was the youngest journalist to win a Pulitzer Prize for editorial writing when he worked for the *Boston Herald*; he was a former writer for Time magazine; he was a published novelist and poet; and he had been a World War II paratrooper on the European front.

But his life's work — work that eventually got him referred to as America's greatest writing teacher — was having the patience, the skill, the caring and the love to teach anyone who was willing to work to be a writer.

Everything about Murray's course was a shock. No textbook. No long lectures. We were not treated as empty vessels obediently awaiting his wisdom, although he had more of that than any man or woman I ever met. From day one, we were writers. From day one, we wrote, right there in class, without being told in any great pedantic detail what to write or how to write.

Murray had hung a motto for the course on the back wall, a quote from the 19th-century novelist Robert Louis Stevenson: "A man who knew how to omit would make an ILIAD of a daily paper." It took me awhile to get that, but with time and Murray's teaching — in the classroom and in the weekly one-on-ones we had with him — I came to understand the great lesson in writing expressed in those 15 words on the wall.

Writing was re-writing. Writing was work. Writing was being willing to get rid of all the bad writing. More words, bigger words, abstract words — the sort of writing rewarded by high school English teachers — was bad writing. Good writers "omit" that stuff. Good writers write for readers. Good writers write to be understood, not to impress.

Murray would read good writing in class. He'd show us his own drafts, his own errors. In the individual sessions — which scared me to hell, having to talk to a professor like he was just another human being — he did not mark up your work in red, did not give it a grade. He talked to you about your writing as if you were, like him, a writer.

Write about your own experiences, he'd say, about the people you know, the places you've been.

My early writing — essays about my sports car, passing time at the laundro-mat, crazy camping trips with Mack and the gang — was likely shit, but he'd always find something good in them, and what he found worth commenting on taught me how to write: to be concrete; to value nouns and verbs, not flabby adjectives and adverbs; to find the right word, not the almost-right word. He taught me that writing was a process — not a mystery. Sure, some great writers were born artists; but writing was also a craft, a craft that someone who wasn't a natural could master with hard work and practice, practice, practice.

Writing wasn't magically produced by inspiration. It was just as hard as all those jobs I worked at to earn money for school. Probably harder. But Murray himself was an inspiration. He believed in words and sentences and paragraphs and spoke of them so passionately that, as Yeats wrote of the great poets, "one believed he had a sword upstairs."

You, he said, you shy teenager who the nuns said couldn't make it in col-lege — you can be a writer.

You, the big-sweatered girl from the little White Mountains village, away from home for the first time — yes, you can write.

I know writers, he said. I am a writer. I'll write with you, and we'll both be writers.

Instead of a grade on every paper, Murray gave a final grade based on two factors: 1. Whether you did all the work, and there was a lot of it, so much that a friend of mine quit the class saying, "Who does he think he is. He acts like his is the only course we take"; and 2. If you improved as the semester went on. If you started, say, as a one on a scale of 10, and got up to a four or five, you'd get as good a grade as the student who came in at five or six and got up to a nine.

I never missed one of his classes and left every one excited to get the words right, to write to discover what I had to say, to maybe, maybe, maybe achieve — some day — a new identity: writer.

As far as I could tell, Murray took a personal interest in all his students, and I didn't think the questions about my family and background that he asked in the individual sessions were anything unusual for him. He knew I came from Dover, that my parents worked in factories, that I had gone to a Catholic high school and that I had just begun living on campus. But I was sure he knew at least as much about his other students, and much more about the core of Murray loyalists who took all five of his courses. I was just in his elementary writing course. The real writers and future journalists were in news writing and advanced non-fiction writing classes. So he had many students with whom he probably had a deeper and longer relationship than he did with me. He also advised the school newspaper and had his own writing (he was about to publish the first of a dozen-plus books on the teaching of writing).

I had begun to see him in a way I had never seen a teacher, or, for that matter, any adult. My experience until then with teachers was transactional: The teachers knew things I didn't know; if I paid attention and did the work, I would know them too (the major theme in The Scarlet Letter, the equation for the isosceles triangle, the difference between macro- and micro-economics). Get a grade, hope to remember some of that stuff, end of class, end of story.

Not so with Donald M. Murray. He paid attention to me and expected the same in return. And that was new, too — he expected something from me. Effort. Improvement. Enthusiasm.

"This is a good start, but do another rewrite. You can do better, John."

I won't call Murray my mentor or a role model because he would object — as I learned to object — to these lazy terms. "Show, don't tell," he'd say. He collected quotations from the great writers and one from Mark Twain has always stuck with me: "Don't say the old lady screamed — bring her on and let her scream."

So I won't "say" what Don Murray did a few days after Christmas 1967. I'll just bring him on.

• • •

On Saturday morning, Dec. 30, 1967, I was home from UNH for the Christmas vacation. I slept in that morning because I'd been out late the night before with Mack, who was also home from college. Mom was home, but Dad was working an overtime shift.

I wish I remembered all the details of what happened, but it was a blur then and it is now. A phone call, a scream from my mother and the simple statement that your father is dead. He had a heart attack at work. They brought him to the hospital, but it was too late.

The next thing I remember is cars arriving, their tires crunching over the icy ruts in the driveway, and Army Mae sobbing and saying, "I can't believe Tommy is gone." Gary was just stunned, silent, mostly staying in his room.

I didn't know how to react. I had finally broken free of being the good boy and liked it. I had a girlfriend. I had pals. I lived in a dorm with people not like me — a roommate who'd gone to prep school; hockey players from Boston; a Jewish guy from New York. I even had friends who were married with a kid. I didn't think I needed a father or a mother. It was sad and tragic that my dad had died on the factory floor, but my grief and shock were waging a battle with the new, independent me. I just couldn't allow myself to feel — anything, really.

I might have been more shaken if I'd stopped to wonder how I was going to pay for my college tuition and room and board. Even though I worked summers and after school, that just kept me in spending and gas money. The bulk of the cost of keeping me in school came from Mom and Dad.

I didn't know then what they made, but I must have realized it wasn't much, for why else would they both have worked overtime at such demanding jobs.

Twenty-five years later, when my mother died and I was going through her records, I found my parents' tax return from 1967, the last year there were two incomes in the Christie family. Dad made $6,866.57, or $132 a week, and that included some weeks he worked more than 40 hours. Mom made $4,437.43, or $85 a week, also including overtime. That's all before deductions for federal income taxes and Social Security.

Their total "take home" income was $9,344 for the year — just a bit below the average income for a family of four in New Hampshire. But, with Dad's death and just my mother's income, the Christie household income dropped to about $4,500. In today's dollars, that's $27,000 — just 33 percent above the poverty level. There was a bit of income from Social Security death benefits, and Dad had a small life insurance policy, but there was still nowhere near enough money to make up for the income from Dad's job.

On Monday, Jan. 2, 1968 — a day after I turned 20 — the local newspaper published the obituary for Thomas H. Christie, age 58. Don Murray read the Dover paper. Don Murray didn't need to see my parents' tax return to recognize the problem I was still too naïve or clueless to see for myself.

The funeral had been that morning, and when the call came every aunt and uncle, cousin and old family friend was jammed into our little Cape, drinking coffee, smoking their Luckys and Camels.

Army Mae was the hoverer that day, the one who kept busy taking away the dirty cups and saucers, emptying the ashtrays and looking out the window to announce who was coming up the walkway. When the wall phone in the kitchen rang, this aunt of mine felt it was her duty to pick it up with alacrity.

"Quod, it's for you."

"Who is it?"

"I don't know who it is. I've never heard that voice before. He asked for Mrs. Christie." All said in a tone of incredulity, for we lived in a world where only people we knew called us on the phone.

Everyone stopped talking. They set their coffee cups down on the table without a clink.

My mother took the call and said very little but spoke in a formal way that was her attempt to sound like the refined lady she wished she could have been. There were lots of "Yes, oh thank you very much" and "That's very nice of you" but no clues to the identity of this mystery caller who required such deference.

When she hung up the phone, my normally inquisitive relatives still didn't say a word. It was like waiting for the answer to the $64,000 question.

"It was John's professor in Durham, Mr. Murray."

Oh-oh, I thought. He's calling to say I flunked the course, or I forgot to hand in a paper. I thought only high school teachers did that stuff.

"He heard about Tommy dying and he wanted to make sure we had enough money to keep John in school," my mother said. "I never heard of such a thing — a professor calling about one student."

Army Mae finally spoke: "Didya hear that? That was Johnny's professor.

He called us at home."

Mysteriously, when I went back to UNH I had been given a tuition grant good until I graduated. Between what I could earn as a part-time janitor at Dover High School, summer jobs and, later, as a paid staff member of the university newspaper, and what my mother could give me from her Social Security, I made it through UNH with only a small loan.

And, from that moment on, I joined the Murray loyalists, taking every one of his courses, which led to a tryout at the school newspaper and a career as a newspaperman: reporter, editor, publisher at newspapers in Maine, Massachusetts and Florida.

By the end of the semester, my writing had improved, which to another teacher might have seemed meaningless because, having started out at such a low level, it was still self-conscious and awkward. But Murray had seen that I not only did every assignment, I was eager for the challenge. For the first time in my life as a student, I wanted to do the work, I wanted to do well for its own sake, not for a grade.

Was the desire to write always there, a low flicker that needed a Murray to turn up the gas? Or had I been waiting for a teacher who believed in me, who expected something from me, and I was just plain lucky it turned out to be the country's premier teacher of writing?

As little promise as I showed, there must have been enough there for Murray to worry, when he read Dad's obit, that my chance to be a writer was about to be snuffed out. So he made that call that lived on as legend in my family. It ensured that what had begun in Expository Writing would not end when my father grasped his chest and fell to the floor in the giant mill in the heart of Dover.

Becoming a writer and editor not only gave me a career and a good living (before the internet displaced newspapers), but a love of a craft that allowed me to tell this story.

Cousin Tammy and the author. Photo by John Christie.

CHAPTER 28

Encounter with Tammy

Oh won't you stay
Stay awhile with your own ones
Don't ever stray
Stray so far from your own ones
Cause the world is so cold
Don't care nothing about your soul
You share with your own ones
— Van Morrison, "Irish Heartbeat"

The Tammy tape told a story. But a good reporter knows there's often a story behind the story. What would the story of how and why cousin Tammy made the recording tell me?

To find out I had to track down cousin Tammy. Searching online, I found an address in Hollis, N.H., and mailed her a copy of a story that I had published about Nana and the genocide in the Portland, Maine, Sunday newspaper, much of it based on her recording. I included my email, phone and home address, but never heard back. Maybe she resented that I had used the recording without her permission. Or maybe she had moved.

Then, I looked her up the easy way: Facebook, where she was a frequent flier, and I had a message back right away. She agreed to meet for lunch at the Whole Foods in Manchester, N.H.

I took a seat at the grocery store's pub —"Goffee's Watering Hole." While Creedence Clearwater Revival and Rod Stewart poured down from the overhead speakers, I wondered if a place so overflowing with food for the discerning consumer was the right place to talk about a woman who would "never, never" forget that her baby brother had died of starvation.

But as I waited for Tammy, I decided I didn't care so much about the venue. I just hoped she would show up and would not resent my reporter-like probing.

I had no idea what she looked like. I hadn't even tried to figure out her age. Her full name was Tammy Fareed, and I knew that it was her mother who was Armenian while her father, I vaguely recalled, was Egyptian and a university economist. I half expected an exotic-looking Middle Eastern woman, much younger than me, with the sophisticated look of an academic.

When she approached my table I saw an attractive woman dressed for a New Hampshire winter day: a pretty heathery sweater over a maroon tee-shirt, dark slacks, gray-streaked hair pulled back, tiny earrings and a pair of glasses with red frames.

It was not, however, a New England face: The full lips, the strong chin, the almost-olive complexion said she was, as we say in New England, "from away." I took a selfie of the two of us and sent it a few days later to my Aunt Lity in California whose assessment was: "She looks just like Nana!!!" It wasn't so much any individual features Lity was responding to, more the overall look and expression.

I began by thanking Tammy for making the recording, letting her know that without it I probably didn't have a foundation for the book I wanted to write. Her interview was hardly the work of a student; she'd had the good sense to ask a few key questions and then get out of the way and let Nana speak, which is what I hoped I would have done. I was curious about what had led her to interview Nana, a woman I discovered she barely knew.

At first, she said she didn't precisely remember why she made the recording, recalling that around 1989-90 she'd had a break between internships and it occurred to her that she could drive from Delaware, where she had been living, to Dover "to visit Aunt Rose," whom she hadn't seen in decades.

"What got that bee in my bonnet? Was it the anniversary of the Statue of Liberty?" she wondered, and then tried to answer her own question.

"There was a series of prompts having to do with immigration, the family, and another prompt was in my heart, was that growing up I knew nothing about my mother ... I knew little snippets, but not much ... In any case, at some point I realized I knew nothing about my mother and I knew nothing about her family and that meant I knew nothing about half of myself ..."

That I got.

Tammy was another searcher of the past, hoping that what she found would explain her to herself.

As we talked I heard a tale that did not fit anything I knew about the Hovsepians of Suedia.

One of the Hovsepians was Nana's brother, Joseph. Nana barely mentions him on the tape, and I don't recall ever hearing a word about him. But Tammy had some of Joseph's story, because Joseph was her grandfather.

Tammy doesn't say — or perhaps didn't know — how Joseph escaped the genocide. But, like his sister Gulenia, he made his way to Cairo, likely around 1915. At one point, he tried to immigrate to Brazil, but officials there wouldn't let him off the boat, and he returned to live the rest of his life in Cairo. Here, a character from Nana's story reappears: the rescuer of her and her sister Violet — one Uncle George.

Tammy brought out an envelope and said she had brought some family photos to share, including one of George Yusef Antaki, brother of Nana's murdered father. The hero of Nana's story, the man who could rescue orphans from a murderous empire, in one quick moment was about to go from legend to reality.

The photo did not disappoint.

Uncle George was an imposing figure with a tasseled fez atop a head like a monument and a mustache for the ages, groomed to an upward twist at the ends.

George hadn't stopped rescuing lost Armenians after he saved Gulenia and Violet. He and his wife (he got married at some point) adopted an Armenian girl named Angel from an orphanage somewhere in the Ottoman Empire near the end of WWI.

George brought Angel home to live with him and his wife in Cairo. But he had also taken in Joseph, who was some years older than Angel, probably in his late teens.

Joseph "had an extraordinarily horrible reputation," Tammy said. Uncle George did his best for Joseph, but he was "always in trouble," and he wouldn't leave little Angel alone. "Basically, for two or three years they try to keep him off her" and when she is a few years older — Tammy isn't sure exactly how old — Uncle George forced Joseph to marry Angel.

Joseph never makes much of a living, working at one time doing deliveries from a druggist, and whatever he makes he gambles and drinks away. Uncle George's wife is suspicious of his wanderings and one day secretly follows him and discovers he is having an affair with a married woman in the neighborhood.

All this is old news to Tammy, whose mother, Helen, is the child of Joseph and Angel. But not only is it fresh news for me, it is also unlike anything I have ever heard or expected to hear about the Armenian side of my family. Sure, Licky had a drink at the Elks Club, went to the track and, as a single man, had a girl friend or two. But he also lived with his mother, had a steady job his whole life and — like everyone I grew up with — never had a scandal or even came close.

I had wanted to meet Tammy, hear her story, because she was my connection to Nana's story — and perhaps more. Until she was five years old and moved to the U. S. with her mother (her father was already here studying economics at Vanderbilt University), she had lived with or close to Joseph, her grandfather. Joseph, it turned out, was Nana's black sheep brother, but a brother still, who experienced the same tragedy and trauma Nana and her other brothers and sisters had. He was there, too, when Elias Hovsepian took his weapons and went to confront the Turks who had come for the Armenians.

I asked Tammy why she thought Joseph was so different from what I knew of the rest of the family and the Armenian reputation for rectitude.

"My mother said in recent years she believes he was traumatized by what he saw in Armenia … it tore his family apart and forced him from something of an idyllic home into the foreign, urban life of Cairo," she said. "His father killed, his mother dead, living with poor relatives in tenements, a refugee and a Christian (Christians were not troubled in Egypt at the time, but they were definitely seen as second-class citizens). Rose, of course, found a way to survive and thrive wherever she found herself."

As the lunch was coming to an end, we shared more family pictures. Tammy leafed through mine until she saw the photo of Nana holding me in her lap in her iron grip. She stopped and studied it intently and a warmth and wistfulness I had not seen until then came over her.

"Oh, that's Rose, right? And that's you?"

"Yes," I said, "Doesn't she look sad," which is how I had always interpreted her expression.

"No, she doesn't look sad at all," Tammy replied. "She does look troubled. She looks determined. And she's also watching, she's examining, paying attention."

Tammy had met my grandmother only a few times, but because of her own family history it didn't take her long to size her up:

"Nobody," Tammy said, still gazing at the photo, "was messing with Aunt Rose."

I hadn't ever quite seen her that way, but Tammy was onto something that helped me see myself in a fresh light.

When I left working class Dover and went on to college and then to a career in publishing, I came to know dozens, hundreds of colleagues, friends, acquaintances who came from much less humble backgrounds than I had. We would trade family stories. This one's father was a marine architect. That one's uncle went to an Ivy League college. Another had an MBA from Harvard and worked in finance. Even friends whose parents had been high school teachers or nurses or low-level managers came from families of greater affluence with more professional credentials than mine. My grandparents were immigrants who never had the chance to get an education, never worked at anything better than factory jobs. It was pretty much the same for my parents: Dad quit school at age 16 to work in the mill, and my mother spent a lifetime assembling electric meters. The story of the immigrant who worked his way through college or began a thriving business is a pillar of the American identity. But that's not how things were in my family.

I wasn't embarrassed or ashamed of them. They were honorable, upstanding people who expected me to adhere to the same standards. But whenever I heard about the status and success achieved by the families of my friends I felt diminished, out of place, inferior, and I continued to feel that way even after I myself had achieved the kind of job titles, professional honors and financial success that should have insulated me against such feelings of insecurity. That was part of what had made me so uncomfortable at Naomi's children's camp.

Tammy's immediate and intuitive description of Nana opened up a more expansive, generous self-narrative. No fancy degrees, no big bank accounts, no names on buildings hung on my family's tree; but my veins coursed with the blood of a woman who defied the attempts of a literal empire to kill her.

"You didn't mess with Nana" was right.

When I grew out of the protection of my family, left behind the insularity of the gang and graduated from the college bubble, I had to do what everyone new to the adult world does: make my way on my own. I didn't have to escape from murderous Turks, but a bit of the "don't mess with me" attitude stood me well as a young newspaper reporter out to prove himself. The best way to get the full story about an antiwar riot was to put myself in the middle of the rioters and risk getting trampled or a baton across the knees. The Gloucester, Mass., police department took me to court to try to get me to give the name of a confidential source who helped me expose a pattern of police brutality. A local judge ordered me to violate my promise to the source, who was afraid the police would harm her based on her having seen them beat up other people. I refused the judge's order and was one day from being sent to jail for contempt of court when a federal judge intervened and overruled the local judge. One of the angry cops then threatened to burn down my house.

I should have been scared or intimidated, but for no reason I could explain back then, I wasn't. It pissed me off that the city thought it could force me to reveal a source. I wanted to find that cop and tell him to his face to back off.

When the police department lost its case in court, they tried another tack. They turned the tables on me, sending a detective to Dover to see what they could dig up to discredit my reporting.

A friendly source in the department told me the detective found only one incriminating fact. That Irish last name of mine? It didn't tell the whole story. I had been hiding something.

"They found out," my source told me, "that you're really an Armenian."

• • •

Yes, I am, and for that I thank my Nana and her children, for without them I would not have a story to tell.

Without my mother and father, I would not have been cared for so well, nor had the money to go to college and become the writer who could tell this story.

Without Mack and the gang, I would not have gained the confidence to step into the world — rather than to wait meekly on the sidelines — and become the reporter who one day could report on his own story.

Without Tammy and her tape, I would not have had many of the details I needed to flesh out the story.

Without all of them, I would not have found the answer to the first question in the Baltimore Catechism: "Who made me?"

The answer in the Baltimore Catechism is "God made me." But I was really made on a dead-end street in Dover, N.H., by a family of Armenians and one Irishman. And on Henry Law Avenue by a gang of wild boys. And on a college campus by a big-hearted man of words.

All of them are my own ones, the ones I share a soul with.

Nick Christie gesturing to a pasture in Bitias, Turkey, that we believed was very much like the one near Nana's home there more than 100 years ago. Photo by John Christie.

CHAPTER 29

Return to Suedia

In the months after the trip to the canoe camp in Canada, I experienced some shorter but still debilitating feelings of regret, disloyalty and dissociation. But, with time, Naomi's patience, therapy and self-examination, they faded.

I had come to know that of all the possible motivations of human behavior, the one that drives me most is loyalty. When I was disloyal — or thought others would think I was being disloyal to them — guilt consumed me. If I had not been as loyal as I believed I should be, as true to those to whom I owe so much, then that dark forest looked awfully inviting.

Those feelings had been transformed into a yearning to express my gratitude to the people I owe my loyalty to, to express it in these words.

And in one final act.

That act was to go back to the beginning, go back to where it all began for Gulenia Hovsepian, my Nana.

I wanted to go to Suedia.

I wanted to go to Nana's home, the home she was forced out of 100 years ago because of her religion, because she was Armenian, and proclaim that I had come in her name.

She herself could never return to her home because her memories were too vivid, her fear too present of what she called — in the only epithet I ever heard her mutter — "those dirty Turks."

And no one else in the family ever wanted to return, either.

The children and grandchildren of other immigrants were making pilgrimages all over the world to discover their roots — going to Irish villages, Greek towns, Ukrainian farmlands. But most Armenian-Americans — including my family — resisted that draw. We never wanted to leave one cent, one breath, one shadow in a country that denied what history has proven: They tried to wipe us out.

Two loyalties were in conflict. If I were loyal to my family's hatred of all things Turkish, I would never go there. But going there would be a defiant form of family loyalty. One took no effort — just stay where I am. The other would mean weeks of planning, considerable expense and, as it turned out, potential danger.

But I couldn't ignore a literal warning sign not go.

That sign was on the U. S. State Department's website about foreign travel. Right there in screaming orange was the "Level three" advisory: "Reconsider travel to Turkey due to terrorism and arbitrary detentions … Terrorist groups continue plotting possible attacks in Turkey. Terrorist organizations explicitly target Western tourists and expatriates."

The only higher warning is Level 4, which included Syria — less than 100 miles away from the section of Turkey where I intended to go.

Naomi was also keeping tabs on the political situation in Turkey, which was under a state of emergency for the elections scheduled to take place in June — just about when I was likely to be there.

Her internet sleuthing turned up a report that the British Foreign Office was advising tourists to stay clear of Istanbul for fear of attacks by Kurdish separatists and ISIS. I couldn't avoid Istanbul; I'd have to go there to get an interior flight to Suedia.

The decision was complicated by the fact that my son, Nick, 37, wanted to go with me. This was a touching offer for Nick to make. For one thing, I would be glad to have a younger, fitter companion with me. For another, while we have always been close — more pals than father/son as he grew into manhood — this experience could deepen that connection. He has no brothers or sisters and his mother, my former wife, died not much more than a year before this trip. Except for a couple great aunts, few cousins and two step-siblings, none whom he sees often, I was all the family he had.

But he has strong memories of my mother and his Uncle Gary, and Nana lived long enough to have spent time with Nick, who remembered his great grandmother "as a caring yet complex woman." One day she was the sweet old nanny patting me on the head and offering me a slice of home-baked apple pie. But on another, she was the fiery competitor yelling, "Who is Mitterand!" at Alex Trebek on her small living room TV.

(She never missed "Jeopardy" and amazed us all with her knowledge of history for a woman who never graduated high school. Maybe we all failed to recognize she knew a lot of history because she had lived it.)

Putting myself in some danger was one thing. I was 70 years old, with many fewer years ahead than Nick, so fewer to put at risk. I couldn't abide the thought of my need to go to Turkey putting my son's life in danger.

I decided to try to find someone with first-hand experience rather than rely solely on the warnings from bureaucrats, who naturally tend to lean towards caution. Through my Aunt Lity (Lillian Goodman), I found out about a tour group called "Historic Armenia."

The group, based in Los Angeles, was led by Annie Kahkejian. Annie, an Armenian, was born in Lebanon and moved to the U.S. in the 70s. She speaks Turkish, Armenian, English and some French and has been to the Suedia area before — in fact, her grandfather was from there.

Her opinion: We will be fine if we don't ask too many questions about the genocide, I don't identify myself as a reporter and we just act like any other tourist.

I consulted with Nick and Naomi.

Taking into account the news, the government warnings, Annie's judgment and what we heard from friends who had been to Turkey (some said don't go; some said, no worries), Nick and I rated our chance of having a problem as five on a scale of 10.

Naomi was not as sanguine, but was somewhat assured when we agreed I'd take precautions like notifying the State Department about our travel plans and, anticipating that we might be questioned by Turkish authorities, removing all references to Armenians and the genocide from my smart phone and taking only innocuous notes.

We were going.

Nick and I contracted with Annie to be our guide, fixer and interpreter in Turkey. She arranged all our hotels and two meals a day there, booked the interior flights we would need and hired a local man to be our driver.

On June 12, 2018, Nick and I met at the international terminal at JFK airport for our nine-hour flight to Istanbul. What had started out more than five years ago as my journey of self-discovery that led me back to my youth, back to my mother and father, back to my Nana and now, back to her beginning, had become not a story of "I." Now, with Nick next to me on the nine-hour plane ride, it was story of "we."

That was unexpected when I began this process, but as I told Nick more of this story, when he read some early drafts, he asked to join me and, as a gift to me, paid most of the expenses. We shared a lot as father and son — a love of baseball, good books and movies and an interest in politics, for example. With this trip, we would have a transformative experience we could share and relive forever.

In our two weeks in Turkey we were never stopped at a checkpoint, although we saw a couple. We were careful not to talk about the genocide, although I slipped up once in an Istanbul restaurant, thinking it was too loud for anyone but Nick, Annie and her husband to hear me. Nick was rightfully upset about it because we'd agreed to keep such conversations discreet.

We may not have had a problem, but that didn't mean Turkey was suddenly just another safe place to travel or live; it's not like taking a vacation in Tuscany. As I wrote this, Turkey was detaining 20 Americans on suspicion they were involved with the 2016 attempted coup of Turkey's authoritarian leader, Recep Erdogan.

Erdogan and his henchmen are not nice people. In May 2017, Americans demanding better treatment of Kurds and Armenians in Turkey protested outside the Turkish ambassador's home in Washington, D.C. Erdogan's local security force went into the street and beat up 11 of the protestors. The State Department condemned their actions as an attack on free speech, which tells you a lot about Turkey's attitude towards anyone who speaks up for minorities in their country, especially Kurds and Armenians.

When we were safely in the air on the way back to JFK, Nick and I could finally acknowledge we had been holding our breaths the whole trip, waiting to be asked by the authorities why were in Turkey. We had a story ready: We're just tourists visiting the land of our ancestors. The fact that our name was Christie and not Banaian or Hovsepian might have meant we wouldn't get any tough follow-up questions. But if we had, we weren't going to try to lie our way around the problem. We had come this far to affirm our family, not deny them.

Our first night in Turkey was spent at a luxury hotel just a couple of blocks from Taksim Square, the nightly gathering place for Istanbul's young people and the site of many political protests. As I was settling in, I had a moment to reflect that Nick and I had overcome some serious reservations to finally find ourselves in the country we never wanted to step foot in so that we could reclaim one of its villages for our family.

If we could find it.

That was the last remaining obstacle to my mission: I didn't know exactly where that village was. I had come to Turkey with a few clues and the hope that what I had not been able to determine from months of research in books and online I could resolve in person.

When my grandmother was asked where she came from, she had the same answer to whoever asked: "Suedia." For the longest time, I could not find it on any maps of Turkey until I came across a map, circa 1900, in an antique shop in, of all places, Savannah. There, in type the size of a cookie crumb, was the name Suedia.

Located in the southernmost district of the Hatay Province of Turkey, Suedia is squeezed between the Syrian border and the Mediterranean Sea. A district — akin to our counties — is not a village. Getting close wasn't going to be good enough. I needed to find her village.

If I could solve that mystery, then I could walk in my Nana's footsteps, run my hands through the mulberry trees, be warmed by the Middle Eastern sun that warmed her and cooled by the breezes off the Mediterranean. I could freely stand in the place where her father was murdered and she and the family were forced to leave simply because they were Armenian, as I am. If she could not go there and say, "You wanted me dead, but I survived," then her grandson — with the same blood coursing through me as coursed through her — could do it for her.

The clues I had were few: Suedia, mulberry trees and a silk factory where the Hovsepians sold the mulberry leaves and where Nana's mother and her siblings hid after Elias was killed.

Annie set our itinerary: Fly to Istanbul, take a flight south the next day to Hatay Airport and then she and her local driver, Seljuk, would take Nick and me further south to Suedia, known now as Samandag, population 35,000.

Arriving in Istanbul, Nick and I took a harrowing taxi ride from the airport and got our first look at this country that for decades I associated with violence, hatred, fear. I knew there was more to Turkey than that, but all I had ever heard, all I had ever read always recalled for me Yeats's phrase "blood-dimmed."

But as the taxi driver wove his way through the traffic, what we saw was fascinating and beautiful. Enormous mosques rising on the hills to our left, their domes as big as stadiums and sprouting multiple minarets like soldier's lances. On our right, a body of water with the fantastical name of Sea of Marmara. Deeper into the city, we passed over the body of water known as The Golden Horn, over the Ataturk Bridge, named after the founder of modern Turkey. All across the country, statues and bridges and parks are named for him. Seeing his name so often reminded me of his history as a murderer of thousands Armenians and our Christian brethren, the Greeks. It reminded me that I should not be lulled to complacency by Istanbul's charms.

As the driver pulled up to our hotel on a tight intersection where taxis, motor scooters and pedestrians calmly maneuvered as if they were not about to collide at any moment, we saw Annie at the hotel entrance. I had only spoken to her on the phone. She retained her middle eastern accent and the confidence — even the assertiveness — I expected from a woman who could wrangle picky tourists, drive a bargain at hotels and restaurants and charm authorities, if it came to that.

And that was exactly what she turned out to be, a vivacious dark-haired woman in her 40s, who seemed to have an endless supply of fashionable, pressed outfits. She was eternally upbeat. Whatever I asked her about, her reply was always the same: 'Of course, Mr. John!'

As were leaving our hotel in Istanbul for the flight, Annie got into a conversation with a middle-aged man in the lobby.

He was Turkish, but not Muslim. He was a minister from a church in Suedia.

"He says there are 28 different villages in Suedia," Annie said, and my heart sank. There was no way in the three days we had scheduled in the district we could explore that many villages.

"But, she said, "there are only six, including Vakifli, where Armenians had ever lived."

Fortuitously, Annie had already arranged for us to stay in a small hotel in Vakifli, because she had been there before and knew it was the only remaining village in Suedia with any Armenians, perhaps 60 or so.

The six villages were all in a valley below Musa Dagh, Moses Mountain. The traditional names of the villages are Yoghunoluk, Kedder Beg, Kabusiye, Haji Habibli, Bitias and Vakifli.

Late on that night in mid-June, after a long drive from Hatay Airport to Samandag, Sanjuk, our driver, maneuvered the Peugeot up the steep and winding road leading to Vakifli, the lowest of the six villages.

Our 10-room hotel sat perched on the western side of the valley, with a balcony from which I got my first view of the past I had been searching for. Samandag lay below us, a dense mosaic of red-tiled roofs back-dropped by a mountain range that bordered Syria. When I looked left, there rose Musa Dagh, and jammed into its slope were the five other once-Armenian villages, each a distinct terraced enclave.

We hadn't found the village yet, but we were in Nana's valley, the place where she was raised. The reporter in me was thinking about next steps, but the grandson in me looked up that lush valley and wished Nana were there with me, and I could have felt her relief and joy at seeing Suedia again.

Exactly 109 years ago, one of those villages was the home of the Hovsepians, who, except for Nana, I knew only by the English translations of their names: Elias, Miriam and their children: Gulenia, Violet, Sara, Joseph and Moses.

Beginning tomorrow, Nick, Annie, Seljuk and I would have three days to find what we were looking for.

The next morning, like all the days we were in Turkey, was hot and hazy, but at least higher up the valley the constant Mediterranean breezes cooled us. We began our day with a surprising breakfast at the hotel's dining area, a dirt floor covered by a louvered roof.

Nick and I had never seen a breakfast like it. I counted 23 items on the table in glazed white dishes: cheeses shaped in tiny balls, or in rectangular slices, in spreads mixed with local spices; olives, black and wrinkled, green and firm, chopped with tomatoes and herbs; yogurt without a touch of sourness, rich and creamy; butter like I had never tasted in my life, like it was made that morning. Endless cups of black tea in tiny, hourglass-shaped glasses.

Midway through eating, the chubby teenage waiter, grandson of the owner, arrived with a copper pan filled with tender scrambled eggs. All through the hour-long feast, two types of flatbread showed up hot from the outdoor oven: one plain, crusty bread the size of a baking sheet; the other round and topped with bright red spices. Seljuk, a fortyish Turkish man in an American golf shirt who spoke no English, would point to each loaf of bread, Nick or I would nod, and he'd tear off a hunk and pass it our way.

Through every good meal we had in Turkey, I thought about the deprivations Gulenia went through as a refugee and an orphan. If, as a boy, I'd be having one of her Toll House cookies and a glass of milk, she'd invariably tell the story of her time in the German Lutheran orphanage.

"Once a year, Johnny, we'd get a glass of milk," she'd say. "You know when? On Kaiser Wilhelm's birthday. That's it. Never again for another whole year."

As we were about to finish breakfast and begin exploring the villages, we were approached by an elderly man in a striped collar shirt and with a welcoming twinkle in his eyes.

Through Annie's translation we found out he was one of the remaining Armenians in Vakifli, Panos Caparyan. He wrote his name down in my notebook along with his birthdate: Jan. 7, 1932, making him 86 years old.

Between cups of tea, Panos took out a wooden flute and played us tunes and then put it down and sang what Annie said was a Armenian patriotic song, all of which he suggested we record with our phones. When the performance was over and we applauded, he spoke his only English words in a singsong lilt: "Thank you very much!"

He was born well after the Hovsepians were forced from their home, but I hoped he might have heard their name or have some other clue that would help us.

He asked my name and to keep it simple, I told him I was a Hovsepian and through Annie asked about any silk factories in the villages.

Annie translated, "Yes, he said there was one in Bitias. It closed in 1939 and all the people from the villages worked there."

Was that the Hovsepians village? Maybe. They could have lived in one of the other villages and walked a distance to the factory with their bundles of leaves. But I also knew from Nana's story that after Elias was killed, Miriam took the family to the factory where the owners hid them until it was safe to come out.

That told me that the factory had to be close to their home. If we could also find mulberry trees there and perhaps a pasture that at least felt right, then maybe we would have found Nana's village.

Panos joined us as we jammed into the Peugeot and Seljuk took off up the steep switchbacks that would lead us up to the five other villages above Vakifli. I had expected something a bit idyllic, simple homes spread apart from each other as would befit a place where most people made their living in agriculture. I expected to smell the blossoms of the orange tree and the briny scent from the Mediterranean.

The first village we saw on the drive, Yoghunoluk, was jammed with local tourists (Ramadan had just ended and it was time for family gatherings and excursions) because in the center of the village stands a legendary tree and tourist attraction: Moses' tree. It is said to have sprouted from the staff the prophet stuck into the ground there more than 2,000 years ago.

A wooden walkway surrounded the tree and a stream rushed through the center of the village, which was ringed by cafes and a farmer's market.

Back on the road, we were glad to have a professional driver in Seljuk. As Nick described it in an email to me after we got back and had time to relive the experience, "the windy, nebulous roads of Musa Dagh were cluttered with chickens, scooters and a surprising number of unattended children who were just as indifferent to our progress as Seljuk was to theirs. Steely faced and muttering in Turkish, he covered ground in minutes that would have taken us hours were we driving alone."

As we approached Bitias, Annie pointed out a series of new, attractive houses built on a hillside with views down the valley to the sea. She said they were being sold to Turks as summer retreats for $100,000. Gentrification had come to what might be Nana's village.

But when we passed those homes and entered the middle of the village, we seemed to have entered the past: Homes built of small, softball-sized stones, turned black and grey over the decades; stucco homes with sheds covered with corrugated metal roofs; the smell of cow manure and wood fires.

Nick and I decided to roam about, with Annie helping to translate if we needed it. Nick had read my transcript of Nana's recollections and knew, as I did, what we were trying to do: to sense, using the few clues we had, that we had found Nana's village or even a house that might have been hers.

We were on the lookout for a building that looked like it had been the silk factory; for mulberry trees; perhaps for a field or a path lined with mulberry trees that we could imagine was the one Gulenia ran through after the Turkish boy told her they were coming to kill the kefirs.

The village and the hills around it were thick with fruit trees and rows of olive trees, but as we walked along the street, paved now in flat interlocking stones, there was never a mulberry tree. No mulberry trees might mean that we were in the wrong place in Suedia altogether.

"There! There!" Annie said, pointing up to a tree at the corner of one of the old stucco homes. "That's a mulberry."

I tore a half dozen of the rough leaves from the tree and stuffed them in a plastic baggie I had brought with me, hoping I could bring back to America a little bit of what Nana had left in Suedia.

Later, we saw other mulberry trees and when we returned to Vakifli, the mayor of the village explained that after the silk factory went of business, villagers stopped cultivating mulberry trees and replaced them with the fruit and olive trees.

The following day, we returned to Bitias.

On the surface, it seemed like just another small Muslim village, with women in head coverings, a minaret poking into the sky, the call to prayer echoing from a loudspeaker.

But the evidence of its Armenian past was still there, literally half-buried: A mosque had been built over the remains of an Armenian church. The Ottoman Turks' plan to purify its empire meant obliterating the offending people and all tangible proof of their existence.

The door to the church was long gone and we were able to walk into what felt like a cellar. It was dark and damp, and when our eyes adjusted from the outside sunlight, we saw the vaulted walls, the baptismal font, the sanctuary, all of it in ruins. The walls green with mold and algae, stone floor ripped up, soda bottle and candy wrappers strewn everywhere, the smell of trash rotting in the dampness.

I was surprised that Nick, who was not raised in any religion, seemed moved and upset; he kept going back to what remained of the baptismal font and asking Annie to translate the Armenian script carved into the walls.

Later, when the three of us roamed up the streets of Bitias, Annie noticed more evidence of the village's origins. She pointed to one of the rounded stones in the wall of an old home.

"See that," she said, "that shape in relief there? That's a cross. Muslim homes don't have crosses on them."

Nick and I kept walking in the village, while Annie and Seljuk rested in the shade of an awning at the local general store. They chatted with an older woman and her adult son, both Muslims, who had lived in the village for years. Annie told them about our quest.

The older woman knew precisely where the silk factory had been. It was just a five-minute walk from the store.

The jumble of one- and two-story concrete buildings with a small interior courtyard was squeezed into a "V" in the road and sat behind a high, green-metal gate. Nick and I walked along the edge of a rock wall and were able to look into the courtyard and see a simple table and chair setup and found what appeared to be two cement tubs that we speculated had been used to wash the mulberry leaves. Now it appeared to be someone's home, although we didn't see anyone there we could talk to.

This, we believed, was where Nana, her mother and siblings hid for hours. They left only after they were told by a local official they would be spared if they walked the 20 miles to Antioch and agreed to stay there with a Muslim family with the expectation that they would convert to Islam.

They followed those orders, but the conversion never happened because some of the family, including Gulenia, escaped. The others were sent to refugee camps and — in Miriam's case — in later years died on a forced march to a concentration camp.

We had found mulberry trees, we had found the silk factory, but our search wasn't over.

Without saying it to each other, Nick and I each knew what we were still looking for: Nana's home. If we looked around enough, if we followed our instincts, could we find a field or house that matched the images we had in our minds of a grove of trees, an old farmhouse, perhaps a stream like the one Elias Hovsepian ran to with his rifle and sabre?

Half an hour later, we stopped just across from a shed where two cows swatted flies with their tails. A few feet below a tumble-down rock wall lay a long stretch of grass, bordered on the uphill side by rows of olive trees — the types of tree the villagers of Bitias planted where there were once mulberry trees.

I started down the uneven rocks, but a rare case of prudence overcame me. If I fell and broke an ankle or worse, the rest of the trip might be over. That's why I had my son who works out every day with me. Nick scrambled down in seconds while I looked on and considered the possibility that we had found what we were looking for.

"This looks just like she described it," Nick said. But unsaid was the fact that we knew that all along the streets of Bitias we could have found other fields like this one.

We stood looking at the scene, took some pictures and felt that we had come as close as we could to the place where the story begins.

If Gulenia did not walk this exact place, if Elias did not run along this precise path to his death, it was a place very close.

Nick walked up and over the rocks to where I waited. We looked back at the field and trees and past them to the slopes of Musa Dagh, getting hazier as the afternoon sun intensified.

We remarked how it probably didn't look a lot different now than it did 100 years ago. But after that, we said little, just stared across the field, and I think shared the feeling that this was a sacred place for our family. Silence

174

was our way of paying our respects.

The next morning, our last morning in the villages, Panos joined us again for tea. I told him we had found the village where the Hovsepians had once lived.

Panos listened as Annie translated.

He put down his cup of tea, lifted his head and addressed me directly.

"Mr. Hovsepian," he said, "you have the face of an Hovsepian."

At that moment, I, John Thomas Christie, never felt more like an Armenian.

I replied with the only English words I was sure he knew: "Thank you very much."

When I returned to the U.S., my wife, my friends and my family all had the same question. How did it make you feel to find what you were looking for?"

I replied that I felt touched and saddened at the time, but now — with more time to reflect — I felt something else.

When I remembered looking up the wide and deep green valley to Bitias and then down to the sliver of turquoise Mediterranean, I felt anger. Life in Bitias was likely hard work for the Hovsepians, but it was home, a home surrounded by mulberry trees and fruit trees, home where their hard work and the land provided them with a place to grow much of their own food, raise cows for milk, yogurt and cheese, bake their own bread on fires stoked by wood they gathered.

I was angry that my Nana was forced from her home for no other reason than she was the wrong religion, the wrong ethnicity. It's a story as old as time. Sometimes, it's the Christians who are disdained, humiliated, jailed, deported, killed. Sometimes it's the Muslims. Sometimes it's the Jews. Sometimes it's the people who are the wrong color, who wear the wrong clothes, who speak the wrong language. It's a story that never ends and goes on even today, in every culture, in every country.

Looking up at her village, I could picture my Nana there as the nine-year-old girl who went to gather the cows, who ran through a field of grass and trees, an innocent child unaware she was only moments away from losing that innocence and her home forever.

Gulenia Hovsepian, later Rose Banaian, later Nana, survived another 87 years, had six children, seven grandchildren and 10 great-grandchildren.

One hundred and ten years after the Ottoman Turks came to kill the infidels of Bitias, two of those descendants — a grandson and a great grandson

— found her home.

By our presence, we had proclaimed that she survived.
They could not kill her.
They could not erase her or her family.
We were proof of that.

A mulberry I left on Nana's gravestone, Pine Hill Cemetery, Dover, N.H. Photo by John Christie.

Epilogue

A few weeks after returning to the U.S., I drove to Pine Hill Cemetery in Dover. In 1995, Nana was buried there in the shadow of a tall spruce.

I slipped one of the mulberry leaves I had gathered in Bitias out of my notebook. I set it on her gravestone, securing it with a rock.

I stepped back and took in the scene: Nana's name engraved on the stone, the mulberry leaf and the ground below me where her body lay. In my journey from America to Turkey and back again, I had acted as the reporter I had been my whole career: observing, questioning, recording. When I had felt like dropping to my knees and weeping, I had resisted. I had to stay on task.

But now the mission was over. The last stage had been bringing the mulberry leaf to Nana.

My breath quickened and the tears came unbidden. And all I could think, all I could say was, "Nana, here's that leaf that tickled your cheeks when you were a little girl about to lose everything. Nana, I'm here, and I'm sorry."

THE END

Bibliography

For more reading about the Armenian Genocide:

Aftandilian, Gregory *The impact of the Armenian Genocide on the offspring of Ottoman Armenian Survivors*. Journal of the Society for Armenian Studies, V. 27.

Balakian, Peter *The Burning Tigris: The Armenian Genocide and America's Response*. Perennial

Balakian, Peter *Black Dog of Fate: An American Son Uncovers His Armenian Past*. Basic Books

Shemmessian, Vahram L. *The Musa Dagh Armenians: A Socioeconomic and Cultural History, 1919-1939*. Haigazian University Press

Simonyan, Hrachik T*he Destruction of Armenians in Cilicia, April 1909*. Gomidas Institute

Werfel, Franz *The Forty Days of Musa Dagh*. The Modern Library

Among the many memoirs I read preparing to write mine, these were the most inspiring:

Baker, Russell *Growing Up*. Congdon & Weed, Inc.

Hochschild, Adam *Half the Way Home: A Memoir of Father and Son*. Syracuse University Press

King, Stephen *On Writing: A Memoir of the Craft*. Pocket Books

Russo, Richard *Elsewhere: A Memoir*. Knopf

Wolfe, Geoffrey *The Duke of Deception: Memories of My Father*. Random House

Wood, Monica *When We Were the Kennedys: A Memoir from Mexico, Maine*. Mariner